Appreciation for *A Happy Truth*

Daisy Hickman's latest book is a heartwarming story for readers who have loved and lost a pet, yet felt uncertain about committing to the next one. *Do I have the courage to love again,* in other words? Via tender stories and poignant reflections on the connection between humans and animals, the author illuminates the gifts of wisdom our four-legged friends are eager to bestow on us.

—Heidi C. Barr, author of *Woodland Manitou* and *Cold Spring Hallelujah*

Eloquent wisdom meets the heart of beloved animals. A compassionate, whimsical and hearty read. A poetic dancer on the page, Daisy A. Hickman leads us back to ourselves through six special beings that are part of the family, *holding space for all of changing life,* through loss, joy, and the inevitable final moments. Each dog, each cat, brings a new version of acceptance and love into our lives.

—Chloe Rachel Gallaway, author of *The Soulful Child: Twelve Years in The Wilderness*

Daisy Hickman offers a conscious approach to understanding the human connection with dogs and cats and urges us to be aware of the faithful affection they share with us. Sifting through the world of literature to share the resonance that others have felt for animals throughout the ages, we learn that Hickman is a keen observer of social intelligence and the best sort of human who is grateful for the magic, warmth and happiness of animals.

—Jacqueline Sheehan, Ph.D., New York Times bestselling novelist, author of *Lost and Found*

The stories in this book are the necessary kind. The enduring bond between human and animal is a reliable source of hope. D. Hickman captures that hope brilliantly in *A Happy Truth*.

—Kelly Butler, Art Editor, *The Southeast Review*, Assistant Poetry Editor, *Narrative Magazine*

A Happy Truth shares poignant and smile-provoking reflections about the special relationships humans share with animals. The perfect book for readers endeared by the quirks of their favorite dog or cat—people who value their joy and Zen-like contentment, and who instinctively connect with these beautiful creatures. While this is a captivating story about the animals the author treasures, it's also a book about life, love, and loss, and how we must embrace all of it.

—C. Lee McKenzie, author of *Sliding on the Edge*

Author Daisy A. Hickman knows the only life worth living is one filled with love, even though loss is always part of the calculation. Dogs and cats, with lifespans that nowhere near mirror ours, almost accidentally, teach us about radical acceptance. Hickman's engaging memoir is one of joy and revelation. While death and loss are byproducts, so are inspiring new beginnings. A loving book from a woman who knows the answer is to take chances, love more, and always, always . . . get another dog.

—Ellen Stimson, author of *Mud Season*

On its surface, *A Happy Truth* tells the story of the life and times of the four dogs and two cats that found a home with the author and her husband. With each twist and turn of phrase, the author weaves a vivid tapestry, adorned with nuances and subtleties too often missed or taken for granted. Carried along as the story unfolds, this joyful memoir encourages us to slow down—zoom in on the meaningful details.

Hickman's writing flows like a warm breeze across open plains on a summer afternoon. But it's so much more. Drawn into the story line with a gentle, never insistent touch, you'll also find yourself traveling in deeper waters. With a mesmerizing sleight of hand, the author dips behind the obvious to pull us closer.

Like *The Silence of Morning,* another gem by the author, *A Happy Truth* is part memoir, part philosophical inquiry. Pet lover or not, read this engaging chronicle. You will not only grow in appreciation for animals, but life itself.

—Dorothy Sander, author of *Life Transitions: The Pathway to a Happier You*

In prior memoirs, *The Silence of Morning: A Memoir of Time Undone* and *Always Returning: The Wisdom of Place,* Daisy Hickman captured readers' hearts with her inimitable writing style. *A Happy Truth* again reveals the author's gift for lyrical prose as she paints a beautiful expression of love between animals and humans. Reading this fascinating story, my imagination was instantly drawn in, even to the exclusion of the outside world. Animal lovers will discover a sense of magic in these pages, and not-yet animal lovers, will be converted. As Hickman suggests: "Caring for them is also a gift in disguise; it's not optional. Their needs can motivate and inspire us to keep moving. Keep breathing, at a minimum."

—Sherrey Meyer, Writer, Blogger, Loving Feline Owner

A multi-layered story, *A Happy Truth* is told in a warm, conversational style. While delighting your heart, it will provoke memories of childhood pets, take you along for happy times and terrifically sad, personality reveals of six furry main characters—Sidney, Lola, Noah, Orion, Hannah, Georgia—with names bestowed on each after much consideration, and lives that enrich the author and her husband's life. We are invited to see these precious family members with new eyes. Are they, when we are receptive, our teachers—guides to enjoying life more fully, being present, trusting, loving, and accepting when we must face steep challenges? How then, do we honor these generous beings?

—Audrey Denecke, Leader Coach,
Senior Organization Development Consultant

A Happy Truth

A Happy Truth

Last Dogs Aren't Always Last

D. A. HICKMAN

CAPTURING MORNING PRESS

Published by
Capturing Morning Press

Copyright © 2019
by Daisy Ann Hickman

All rights reserved

No part of this book may be reproduced or utilized in any form or by any means, electronic or mechanical, including photocopying, recording, or by any information storage or retrieval system, without specific permission from the publisher.

978-0-9908423-9-2 (Print)
978-0-9908423-0-9 (eBook)

Produced in the United States of America

First Edition

capturingmorningpress.com
CMP@capturingmorningpress.com

Logo design and book cover concept
© EKM

Author Photograph
© Erica Lynn

Book and cover design
Michele DeFilippo @ 1106 Design.com

Cover photograph: Clouds at Sunset and Stars
© Javier Pardina, Lleida, Spain

Hannah and Spinach
© D.A. Hickman

So they have graced our path . . .
four spirited dogs and two clever cats
. . . they are all "a happy truth"
Noah, Orion, Hannah, Georgia
Sidney, Lola

Until one has loved an animal,
a part of one's soul remains unawakened.
—ANATOLE FRANCE

ALSO BY DAISY (D.A.) HICKMAN

Ancients of the Earth:
Poems of Time

The Silence of Morning:
A Memoir of Time Undone

Always Returning:
The Wisdom of Place
(Second edition, *Heart Resides*)

Where the Heart Resides:
Timeless Wisdom of the American Prairie

Lucidity

Left to sit with my dog,
us resting on the sandy shore
meditating on sleek schools
of fish hidden from view,
I touched his thinning silver coat
to let him know the current
would never sweep him away,
not if I could help it,
not while the world slept,
oblivious to the affection an animal
is eager to give, even when dumped
by the side of a remote gravel road
like a cheap trinket from a garage sale.

Still motionless, we stared at anything
and everything, a deep resonance
bridging water and sky,
capturing an exquisite harmony.

—D. A. Hickman
Red Coyote Journal, 2018

The world is full of magic things,
patiently waiting for our senses to grow sharper.
—WILLIAM BUTLER YEATS

. . . *a special preface*

DEAR DOG and CAT:

I love you because you are part of our family, not because you are a pedigree, a trendy designer breed, or sport a fancy name and a high-maintenance look. If you were once a stray cat or a rescue dog, that's all behind you. You have a home now. A place to call your own. Humans to care for you, play with you, and feed you. Maybe another cat or dog to run around with, cuddle up with. At our house, dogs and cats love our window seat with a cushioned ledge for napping or observing the fascinating world beyond. People coming and going. Rabbits, squirrels, birds in flight. Neighborhood dogs and cats. Children on bikes, parents with strollers. All interesting, isn't it?

A window seat is a great place to gaze at the natural world, but it's also a gathering place for you and your four-legged companions. A cozy spot to see what's going on or wait for our return. A place to catch the morning sun. Maybe you need a quiet moment to chew on an old sock or shoe, yet unfailingly pausing to greet other dogs out for a walk.

Whatever you choose to do, it's your place to relax, to dream about treats or playing fetch or going for a car ride.

I wish every dog and cat had a special place to study nature and passersby, to sing (howl or bark), and to gaze at thick clouds threatening rain, winter snowfall, or trees in motion from strong winds. Home should be a place where you feel safe, loved, and comfortable. We're so glad you're here. Life would be strangely quiet, way too dull and orderly, without you. Your gentle companionship, spontaneity, and playful ways would be sorely missed.

Thank you for sharing your priceless gifts, your brief time on Earth, with us. If lucky, we'll grow old with you at our side. Collectively, **you** are the small steps that echo our lives—that make each moment more meaningful and purposeful. Because of you, in the eloquent words of Elizabeth Barrett Browning, my sun sets to rise again.

CONTENTS

Let Hercules himself do what he may,
The cat will mew and dog will have his day.

—WILLIAM SHAKESPEARE

FOREWORD	xix
PROLOGUE	xxiii

Part One: NOTHING TO FEAR

1.	A Visitor	5
2.	Meeting Noah	10
3.	Orion	15
4.	The Grand Scheme	26
5.	Stop Signs	39
6.	Star Gazing	48
7.	Pumpkin Bars	61
8.	Hands of Fate	75
9.	Caught in Reverie	85
10.	Hair on Fire	91
11.	Zen of Noah	102

Part Two: EVERYTHING TO GAIN

12.	Deep-Toned Bell	115
13.	Famous or Not	123
14.	A Small Photograph	128

15.	FINDING HER	133
16.	SHE IS A SHE	144
17.	CARROT CAKE	152
18.	HANNAH'S WINDOW	163
19.	STAR WARS REUNION	178
20.	STARRY NIGHTS	182
21.	SHOWGIRL	188
22.	SLEEPY EYE AND LINUS	196
23.	TENDER MOMENTS	214
24.	THE STILL POINT	223
25.	RING THEM BELLS	229
26.	MAGIC THINGS	240

EPILOGUE	251
ZEN OF NOAH RECAP	253
AUTHOR NOTE	259
WARM THANKS	261
ABOUT THE AUTHOR	263

> *I have known many dogs, and many a story I could tell of their wisdom and devotion; but to none do I owe so much as to Stickeen. At first the least promising and least known of my dog-friends, he suddenly became the best known of them all. Our storm-battle for life brought him to light, and through him as through a window I have ever since been looking with deeper sympathy into all my fellow mortals.*
>
> —JOHN MUIR, "Stickeen" 1909

FOREWORD

After reading *A Happy Truth,* I turned off my computer, hooked a leash to my dog's blue collar and headed into the Arizona evening for a long walk. The sky, as it often does, blazed streaks of sunset orange; the air swirled with the heady fragrance of orange blossoms. Zucca, our miniature poodle of sixteen, has curly black hair mixed with gray. Though cataracts cloud his eyes, and he can barely hear me when I call to him, his puppy spirit remains joyful and, oh, how he still loves his walks.

Never was I so aware of the blessings that Zucca has bestowed on our family as during this walk. Daisy Hickman's new book had reminded me to slow down, drink in the miracle of this furry fellow, and reflect upon what this sixteen-year journey has meant, and continues to mean, to me and my family.

Zucca came into our lives quite unexpectedly. In 2003 we had moved our family of four to Genoa, Italy, for a sabbatical of sorts, and we were feeling displaced and lonely. Late one afternoon, as my fifteen-year-old daughter, Katie, and I were returning from a particularly disturbing doctor's appointment, we glanced through the bus window and spied a tiny pet shop with puppies for sale. Katie asked if we could go look at them.

I didn't see the harm knowing that the diversion would lift our spirits. So, we got off the bus, backtracked to the store, and pressed our noses against the cold glass. Three bundles of fur, the size of softballs, peered back at us. Two were white and one was black. Yes, you guessed it, we left a few minutes later with our barboncino in miniatura.

The second our eyes had connected with his, we knew he had chosen us.

Emotionally, I loved the idea of sweeping him into our arms and carrying him home. Intellectually, however, I suspected it was a terrible decision. I never really considered myself an animal person. Sure, my family had a few great dogs while I was growing up, but I can't say that I bonded with them on a deep level. We were a big, loud family with a lot going on—the dog was merely one more ball of motion thrown into the mix.

That night, I sat up with acute buyer's remorse. A new puppy in a foreign country? Who would train him? Who would walk him? Of course, I knew the answer to my questions: the mom!

I was so afraid of all the negatives, so stressed that it would add one more thing to my to-do list, that I didn't realize he would add so much more to the "what brings us joy" list. What I didn't realize then—what I now know—was how this energetic puppy would awaken a part of my soul that I never knew existed. I would come to cherish him, in fact, and finally understand what it means to truly love an animal though its entire life.

My worries were wasted energy.

We became a tight, loyal pack of five in no time, traversing the back roads of Italy and then, a year later, returning to the States to homes in California and Arizona. Zucca may as well be human, our third child; none of us can imagine life without him.

Animal lovers everywhere delight in sharing the stories about the animals that have graced their lives. Tales of puppyhood, ornery felines, vacation mishaps, and mischievous antics carried out while we ran to the grocery store. We wax poetic about the cherished pet that sits at our feet or on our laps during quiet mornings and lazy summer afternoons. But it is difficult to speak about the way our souls become intertwined with that of our pet's or the depths to which these animals enrich us and our homes. The gift of these feelings can rarely be pinned down with words—because how does one capture a language of the heart?

In *A Happy Truth,* the author accomplishes this task.

In her warm manner, Daisy shares many spirited journeys with beloved animals, bringing to life the joys and challenges that pets bring to our days and the lessons we learn from them. Eloquently, she expresses the deep emotional connections we come to share with furry family members.

Daisy also dares to remind us that no matter what age an animal comes to us, in all probability, we will outlive them; a heart-wrenching day will come when we have no choice but to set them free. Unabashedly, she explores that dark space of grief when a beloved animal passes and asks us to consider what it means to start anew with another dog or cat.

Because she has navigated this decision a few times, Daisy reveals how she and her husband, John, decided to bring new cats or dogs into their home and hearts—what she calls: "The curious process of getting to the next dog." (Cat, bird, or horse.) Such personal revelation blazes a path for us to follow; it offers the assurance that the circle of life is as it should be, continuing in unforeseen, and often delightful, twists and turns.

Born in October, *Zucca* is an Italian word meaning pumpkin.

Watching Zucca as he trots along the sidewalk, stopping here and there to sniff and scratch, I know his time with us is limited. A harsh certainty that fills me with an unbearable sorrow. However, I'm buoyed by Daisy's story of four spirited dogs and two clever cats, and know that when the time comes, I will seek her guidance again within the covers of this heartwarming book. For now, though, I will treasure each tender moment with Zucca, while happily giving thanks for the barboncino in miniatura who unexpectedly chose us one quiet afternoon in Genoa.

—Susan Hall Pohlman
Halfway to Each Other:
How a Year in Italy Brought Our Family Home
Scottsdale, Arizona
2019

PROLOGUE
Blaze a Trail

I was the first dog. A salt and pepper schnauzer, my name was Noah. Before I arrived there was a cat named Sidney; a farm cat, he was white with one blue eye, one green, and was rather mischievous. One day, though, after reaching his advanced years, he departed this world of time and ailments, and a mystery kitten named Lola came calling. Mostly white with dabs of gray and tan, we were good pals, and the Lola-Noah years were long and blissful.

Somehow, though, just like everyone, I grew older, as did Lola, and for some reason, everyone thought I could use a feisty puppy to keep me going. That idea led to Orion, a black and silver schnauzer. A rather wild guy, he definitely energized our home and tried his best to befriend me and Lola. For the most part, we all got along, and I really liked brother Orion. We had our small differences, but he encouraged me to play more, sleep less. Lola, like any smart cat, had no problem keeping Orion in line.

Then one day, sadly enough, I was called away to a faraway place where all good dogs go, and Lola and Orion missed me. So one day the third dog idea came to life, but no one could decide if it was the right time or not exactly. This complicated back and forth went on for a while, this indecision about another puppy, one that definitely would be the "last dog." I couldn't figure out what the big deal was, but my family wanted to be super sure about a new dog before taking the plunge.

One day, though, a decision (hallelujah!) was made, and little Hannah, a white schnauzer, and yes, the much-thought-about third dog who also had to follow in my rather impressive footsteps, arrived on the scene.

I don't want to share much more about this story of a "happy truth," but let me gently mention that the Lola, Orion, and Hannah years had some ups and downs—some surprises. And one day, Hannah, the third dog, was all alone.

No one had seen this coming; no one knew exactly what to do. But without Orion and his long silver eyebrows, a handsome guy the same color as a sparkly night sky, quiet musings about a fourth dog crept into dreams, conversations, and meditations.

Could it be that Hannah wasn't the last dog, after all? Between you and me, I've heard murmurings of a playful puppy, a schnauzer, named Georgia. But I can't imagine how that decision was made, and if true, then surely, *she* is the last dog.

But wait, is she?

I'm glad I was the first dog. I started a very good trend, don't you think?

> *Do not go where the path may lead, go instead where there is no path, and leave a trail.*
> —RALPH WALDO EMERSON

A Happy Truth

Part One
NOTHING TO FEAR

Hannah

We are a species that has lost its way.
Everything natural, every flower or tree,
and every animal have important lessons to teach us
if we would only stop, look, and listen.
—ECKHART TOLLE

One

A VISITOR

When we adopted Lola, our second white cat, she belonged to our neighbors in Lake St. Louis, but for mysterious reasons of her own, had taken a keen interest in us. My writing study in those days sat at ground level with a good-sized window to the north. After opening it to savor the warm autumn weather—a light breeze, a sun-filled sky—I'd turned to my work. Diligently, I'd faced my keyboard to grapple with an article I was drafting, but I was also seriously restless: my mind wandering like a wind-tossed kite on a string.

A fresh cup of coffee, a chocolate chip cookie from a new recipe I'd tried the night before, or an invigorating walk on tree-lined sidewalks—one street, set on a steep incline, was good exercise—came to mind, but, truthfully, even a very small cookie sounded irresistible. Who doesn't love extra chocolate chips and toasted walnuts tucked in a sweet, chewy cookie? Still, I hadn't given up hope of sticking with my writing, when a blissful distraction saved me from high-calorie temptations.

Nothing more than a persistent scratching noise, I still couldn't believe my good fortune. *But what was it?* Our backyard was private. Not even a yard, really, it was more of an informal, wooded space, a valley of sorts, with redbud trees, sturdy oaks, and random flowers popping up in spring. Glancing toward the open window, blinds pulled high, and both hands still on my keyboard, I wondered if I was seeing things.

Why, oh, why, would a wild-eyed kitten be clinging to my screen—staring at me like she knew me? Not wanting to spook her, I sat very still, didn't speak.

Her coloring was artistic. A patch of golden tan surrounded one eye, meandered up to her ear; a daring spot of charcoal gray near the other eye resembled a perfect dab of paint: the stroke of an artist's brush. Her tiny nose was solid gray. I also saw a touch of tan on a back leg, a paw marked with another splash of gray. Her tail, the part I could see, sported uneven stripes of tan and gray.

I hadn't seen her back yet, but most everything else was a true white.

Seeing how young she was, I wondered why she was out scouting around a city neighborhood without a collar or a name tag. Was she a she, or, perhaps, a he? I'd assumed female because of her petite frame and soft, plaintive meowing. (Cats, I later learned, emit up to sixteen different vocalizations.) I also presumed a stray, but how had she discovered our quiet cul-de-sac, our house, in particular, and my open window? Was she lost, hungry, hurt, or merely inquisitive?

Slowly lifting my hands from the keyboard, I swiveled in my chair to face her, as she meowed and tried to inch her way farther up the screen. Definitely on the move, I decided to go outside, get a closer look.

Easing myself from my chair, I hurried down the hall and out the door, but as soon as I saw her, I slowed down. Walking toward her one short, quiet step at a time, I tried not to startle her. If she darted into the woods, took off, that would be it. I'd never find her (or him) again. She'd spotted me, though, and sharp eyes traced every move. As I drew closer, she stopped moving, grew still, but made no attempt to jump down or run away.

Whispering words of reassurance, cautiously, I reached out for her. I hoped she would let me hold her, but if frightened, ill or feral, she might try to bite me or dig in with her sharp claws. Seemed unlikely though: *Was she purring?* When I picked her up, held her, the purring, in fact, grew louder. A quiet afternoon with most of our neighbors away for the day, jobs, appointments, and so on, all I could hear in the background was a steady flow of traffic from the nearby interstate.

Stroking her, slowly, gently, I studied her unique markings, her healthy-looking white coat, and after she briefly studied my face, she settled in like this was a long-awaited reunion. Not anxious, restless, or fidgety, my mystery kitten clearly wasn't injured or frightened.

MOST CATS, SO I'VE HEARD, find their owners. Famed science-fiction author, Ursula K. Le Guin (1929–2018), echoed this belief in *No Time to Spare: Thinking About What Matters.* Published in 2017 as a collection of her most enduring blog posts, Le Guin writes, with loving good humor, about the time she had to select a kitten from the local shelter because, sadly, her cat had died and another one had yet to find her.

I'm confident Lola (and, of course, I didn't know her name then) wasn't looking for *me* that day, but admittedly, it feels uncanny when we connect with an animal that seems to know us from the start. More precisely, how was it exactly that I'd found a charming, mostly-white kitten clinging to my office window screen when, recently, our cat, also white, had died?

Mere coincidence, many would argue.

Invariably, but a curious and happy one, nonetheless, because some two months prior, in early September of 2001, only yards from where I stood holding Lola, we'd buried Sidney next to a circle of daffodils that pushed skyward during the warm, rainy days of spring. Originally a thin farm cat mostly unaccustomed to the antics of humans, my son, Matt (still in grade school), when presented with an array of wild barn kittens, had selected Sidney, or Mr. White, as we called him.

Alas, after many strong years, and despite our considerable efforts to extend his feline joys, Sidney's kidneys failed, and the grand clock of time chimed once more. And ever since that fateful day, I'd seen him in ghost-like fashion, perched on the window seat, sleeping on the deck by a pot of red geraniums, so the appearance of a seemingly tenacious kitten that looked like a small version of Sidney was an eerie jolt.

Still holding her, listening to that steady purr, I felt a swirling mix of disbelief, joy, and puzzlement. Trying to gather my thoughts, I could only wonder what to do next. Take her inside, release her, call the humane society, or put an ad in the paper. I loved her at first glance, of course, but that was another issue entirely.

SOMETIMES, THOUGH, as happened to me, the prospect of a new puppy, a new kitten, generates considerable tension that evolves into a marshy tide of indecision. Despite their adorable antics, sweet cuddly ways, *something* holds you back. Loss has come. The dog you had a deep bond with is gone. The beautiful cat that memorized your daily routine, knew your every mood, especially quiet, reflective ones, is gone; and then, many years later, yet another beloved cat departs your world.

Hesitation sets in. Doubts flourish. Excuses flow like steady rain. Inner conflict taunts us, teases us, while keeping us awake well into the night, as fear and worry take root. Too soon? Right time of the year? And, seriously, will our other pets bond with a newcomer? Do we have the time to properly care for a high-energy puppy, a curious kitten—wouldn't an older, well-trained dog be far easier? Or a middle-aged, sleepy feline?

Tension comes and goes, as the decision looms in the background: a slow-moving train, destination unknown. But bringing home a new family member is a *big deal,* and once you've loved a pet, you know it's a significant commitment, not something to rush into without a little soul searching.

Like taking a solemn, albeit joyful, oath to care, love, respect, and spend quality time with until the bitter (and admittedly painful) end, the day may come when signing up for this worthwhile mission feels slightly overwhelming or emotionally risky. Has anxiety entered the picture? Probably.

Are we up to the task *this time?* Do we have the energy? A positive attitude? Doubt and fear go hand in hand, and surprisingly, my typical eagerness to accept the reasonable terms of this mutually beneficial agreement felt distant when the possibility of a new dog, a puppy, gave me serious pause.

Uttering "yes" in years prior had been a relatively routine, pleasant step into the unknown, but things had changed, the roller coaster of life had sped up and intensified, and I felt torn. My sense of inner direction, elusive—a trusted light that refused to shine.

Two

MEETING NOAH

My official "dog days" began with Noah. Like Lola (the kitten found dangling from my window screen), he came to us as a puppy during our time in St. Louis. We'd considered a parade of names. Some lasted a few meager hours, often less; some survived a day or two, before they, too, fell quietly by the wayside. None enlisted our hearts or imagination until I stumbled on Noah.

Wanting to know more about the name, I turned to my computer to learn more, and was pleased to encounter familiar words that resonated: peaceful, builder of the biblical ark, comforter. We didn't know our new dog well, but already, I sensed a special kind of comfort with him. The name, a perfect match.

John, my husband of nearly twenty-four years, is a handsome guy of medium build with oceanic-blue eyes and a short, no-frills haircut that is meant to draw attention from a receding hairline, an impending bald spot. And since my dark hair revealed snow-white strands when I was in my early twenties—thanks to my family tree—we are a good pair. Each of us ahead of our time, you might say.

After studying chemistry at Kenyon College, John opted for a career in sales (scientific equipment); and luckily, since he enjoys travel, meets with clients on a regular basis in several states. Companies and organizations of all sizes linked to a wide variety of industries, but sharing a need for scientific analysis. Since this career choice requires time away from home, we'd talked about the merits of a dog. A smallish dog, easy-going—one that wouldn't frighten our sweet kitten, one of most any kind or color in need of a good home. A cuddly, yet high-spirited dog that loved to take walks or ride in the car.

Certain that amiable canine companionship would be enjoyable, especially when John was on the road, I felt blissfully free of reservations. Without children, teens, or elderly parents living with us, surely, we needed an empty-nest dog. And, as fate would decree, right after we'd come to a firm decision, a call came—homeless puppy needs shelter—that resulted in us welcoming a gray-blonde, four-month-old (best guess) puppy into our home.

Given our conversations about wanting a dog, we knew we would take this puppy sight unseen: for better or for worse, in sickness and in health. No questions asked. A written-in-the-stars, joy-filled connection. We'd verbalized our yearning, after all, and voilà, our modest wish had been granted. Even when it comes to the cats and dogs that grace our lives, the Universe, it seems, conspires with us in mysterious ways, and *certain things* simply happen when meetings and life intersections we never could have planned or predicted materialize almost effortlessly—like gifts.

Heading outside to wait for his arrival, I set aside, as silly, any new-pet concerns, and sat down on our front step under a shade tree. A summer afternoon in June with a light breeze teasing a canopy of oak leaves, it was the kind of day when the world seemed intent on my perpetual happiness. An idyllic moment I wanted to clasp tightly, exchanging it, as needed, for days when things weren't so rosy.

A car turned into our driveway; I stood up, waved. Anxious to see the little guy, I reminded myself to take it slow. The last time I'd cared for an energetic puppy was in the early '80s when my children were young. A different lifetime, surely. Going back even further, during my early years in Pierre, South Dakota, we had a couple of well-loved dogs.

Snoopy, fond of sleeping on the top stair of a carpeted staircase, was difficult to see at night, but we could never seem to remember this, so anyone up and walking around in the dark tripped over him. Laughing about it mostly, he was a gentle soul with a brown and black coat, long, floppy ears, and short legs. He seemed to love us unconditionally. How we found this tireless, good-natured family friend is anyone's guess, but such details don't matter to kids. What mattered to us was that Snoopy was ours to keep and care for, and I hope we did our best.

But, now, Noah was here.

A car door opened and out he came. Small, slightly scraggly—without grooming, it wasn't apparent what sort of dog this was—he was a friendly, eager puppy that seemed to know I'd been waiting for him. As I walked out onto the grass, he tagged behind, and I crouched low to greet him. A shy puppy kiss followed. Instant friends. Relief and joy. Things were going to work out as hoped.

But how did this happy little puppy know this was his new home—that I'd been looking forward to meeting him so much?

I wanted to study his eyes.

Animals, like humans, have eyes that reveal many things; we merely need to pay attention. And this puppy had good eyes. Deep brown, trusting, and perfectly round. Peaceful eyes that grabbed me by the heart, held tight. Fortunately, I didn't detect any fear, anxiety, or aggression, either. Smiling, I offered him my hand for a sniff.

"Hey, little guy, what's your name?" I asked in my best puppy voice.

Long ears perked up as he tipped his head, so I kept talking and slowly reached out to pet him. His coat looked wiry, scruffy and almost thin in places, but I sensed the potential; he was still growing into himself. Establishing trust is of such importance with any cat or dog, so I was glad our initial meeting was low-key, relaxed.

Finally, I stood up, let him sniff around his new yard before taking him inside. Quite naturally, our friendship blossomed and deepened, and even though he was relentless about chasing Lola around the house—*she'd eventually come to live with us, but that's a chapter yet to come*—he was, otherwise, the kind of dog it would be hard not to appreciate. John was on the road when Noah arrived, and even though he'd been slightly more reserved about getting a dog, their first meeting was cordial.

"You look like a good dog," John said, smiling hopefully. Noah, in reply, wagged his tail (short, upright, docked), seemingly agreeable to the "good dog" notion.

Never hurts to mention expectations early in the game, right?

Quietly observing from the sidelines, I could see that John's reasonable concerns about a puppy—the requisite responsibilities, the time commitment—had already slipped away. As it turned out, for good reason. Our new puppy was even-tempered, smart, and playful. He liked everyone he encountered. Increasingly apparent as we got to know him, Noah also possessed a certain charm that made life with him feel inevitable. If we'd looked for a dog for months, we couldn't have found a better dog. Actively searching for one, in fact, could have led to months of tedious vacillation. We might have indefinitely postponed getting a dog and sadly, even given up on the idea.

First Lola, then Noah.

We all benefit from a little serendipity in our lives, don't we?

Three

ORION

"You won't believe what I found online today," I said to John one morning, my voice hovering somewhere between excitement and dismay. July of 2015, the long, steamy days of summer were blossoming, and Noah (2002–2015) was no longer with us. We were down to one dog, Orion, and good-natured Lola. "Someone is selling miniature schnauzer puppies."

Looking at him, I smiled, then sighed . . . my trepidation apparent.

Schnauzer puppies, however, weren't always easy to find, especially since we wouldn't dream of buying one from a pet store. We were also adamant about not supporting, directly or indirectly, inhumane puppy mill situations.

"Hmm," he said, coffee in hand. "I suppose they're cute."

"Seems too early," I said, walking into the kitchen for more butter coffee. "Maybe others will be available when the timing is right." Of course I had no idea when that would be, but it didn't seem like *now*. Pouring coffee into a tall blue mug, I tossed in a slice of grass-fed butter, stirred. We'd given up cream for butter, which made for a healthier morning drink—so we'd read. It was good; we enjoyed it. Super sweet coffee drinks had their place, too, but we'd been down that unruly, sugar-glazed path.

I glanced outside at the birds near our kitchen window feeder. Cardinals. Males. Brilliant red. A couple of females hovered nearby. They loved sunflower seeds, but keeping up with the feeder had evolved into a full-time project. Like the stunning birds, our male dogs, when there were two, were a beautiful pair. Highly attentive watch dogs, spirited companions, that made each day a little brighter and a lot more meaningful. Noah and Orion, beyond their obvious personality differences, clearly were united by their strong "schnauzerly-streak."

"Think I'll crack a window, still nice outside?"

"Pretty morning, cool side so far. So . . . what color are the puppies?" John glanced at me, and before I could reply, he added, "I agree, definitely too soon. Orion seems to love all the extra time and attention he's getting these days."

Standing with his coffee to gaze out the dining room slider—a window featuring an abundance of smudges at the wet-dog-nose level—he was checking on our second schnauzer. Like most animals, Orion loved being outside. I sensed John was imagining a rambunctious puppy running around the yard with him. Just shy of four years, Orion hadn't forgotten his old buddy, Noah.

Whenever his name came up, Orion's head turned, ears perked up, deep brown eyes grew wide, intense. Sometimes, as though searching for his friend, he would hurry to a window or over to the slider to scan the backyard.

Joining John, coffee in hand, we saw Orion slip into high gear to chase a squirrel. Racing along our four-foot fence top—pointed cedar boards, gaps between each—we laughed at the daring squirrel's ballet-like skills.

Orion and John, like soulmates, had clicked the moment their eyes locked. The dead of winter in South Dakota (not a wonderful time of year to house train a puppy), and January, no less, spring was nothing more than a faint, yet fondly remembered rainbow in our minds. But, when John, en route to Minneapolis for work meetings, stopped in a small town along the way to see a seven-week-old male puppy, weather and timing, like yesterday's dream, were soon forgotten. Reminiscent of the special ease and rapport that Noah and I had enjoyed, Orion wanted nothing more than to be near John. Napping, playing, taking a walk, riding in the car, doing nothing at all—it didn't matter to Orion as long as John was in close proximity.

I remember the first picture with John's text: "What do you think? Do we want him?"

The puppy, mostly black with touches of silver and caramel, was the last of his litter. He looked up at John's cell phone as if he knew his hopeful expression could help him win a home. Studying his picture, I was reminded of a song (later, a book) that I'd loved as a girl: "That Doggie in the Window" or "How Much Is That Doggie in the Window?" (words and music by Bob Merrill, 1953).

Smiling, I immediately wrote, "Of course we want him, he's adorable. When can we pick him up? Any names in mind, or does he have one already?"

I loved finding the perfect name. So-so ideas come and go, filtering in and out of consciousness like a tired grocery list, but the *right* name has a certain magic to it, doesn't it?

"No ideas yet," he wrote. "But I can pick him up Friday, on my way back home."

"I'll get puppy food, make sure his crate is set up."

Minutes later, I'd gone looking for Noah and Lola, seniors by then, and blissfully unaware a puppy was coming to live with us. Dozing in a sunny spot near the front door, I didn't disturb them. Wondering how the adjustment period would go, I hoped for the best, but we'd noticed that Noah was slowing down. He'd had his gall bladder removed in late 2010 at the University of Minnesota Veterinarian Medical Center in a life-saving surgery, so he was on a strict, low-fat diet. Seemingly doing well in the aftermath, the months were ticking by, nonetheless.

A cute puppy, I suppose, felt like emotional shelter from the anticipated sorrow of losing Noah one day, but naively, we also thought he might enjoy another dog in his senior years. Companionship, walks together, chasing each other in the yard: a lively puppy generating waves of wild energy to keep Noah engaged.

Our expectations had been only partially right, as they appeared to negotiate a love-hate relationship—emphasis on the canine bond that still grew between them. Noah slept less, played more, and Orion urged him on as we'd hoped, but a puppy's hectic pace was sometimes challenging for Noah. And, unexpectedly, but assuredly, Noah looked saddened by the arrival of a newcomer.

For several months, he avoided my eyes, especially, when I was giving them both attention. Head low, Noah would look away, as if puzzled or bewildered and unable to face this strange new reality. Feeling like a traitor, I hoped he might forgive me, but I also tried to spend more one-on-one time with him—to reassure, and to help him contend with the wiles and star quality of a puppy. A relaxing walk, sitting with him, brushing his unruly locks, taking a nap together, offering a special treat.

Some people doubt that animals and emotions coexist, but it seems we would have to be slightly oblivious to overlook the endless and poignant ways in which they try to share their understanding, awareness, and generous affection with us.

What is a wagging tail, after all? Or that quiet look of appreciation after a good run, or an evening walk?

STILL GAZING OUTSIDE, our eyes trailed Orion. Looking skyward to follow a squawking blue jay or the caw of rowdy crows, each fascinating noise, like a magnet, drew his attention. But, finally, I returned to the topic we were dodging: "Don't know about colors, haven't called yet and the ad didn't specify."

Noah, almost imperceptibly, had blossomed from a bedraggled, yellow-tan puppy into a mature dog wearing his real colors—a soft, gray-white, the apparent source of inquiries and compliments whenever we had him out with us. Admirers would stop us and ask to pet him, or inquire about his name or breed. We heard lots of fun dog stories this way. People who had owned a schnauzer, or several, and couldn't wait to tell us how much Noah reminded them of their dog, or how much they missed their beloved dog, the one they had buried in a special place in their backyard.

I'll never forget the kind woman we ran into one day in St. Charles, Missouri.

Out taking a leisurely walk with Noah when she stopped us, we were enjoying the quaint and historic shopping front adjacent to the Missouri River. Enticing, colorful storefronts lined the old-fashioned brick walk. We'd watched well-planned holiday parades along this street, and sampled several area restaurants. Lewis and Clark was popular. When dining upstairs, the muddy Missouri, the longest river in the United States, that merged with the Mississippi some twenty miles north of St. Louis, was well within view.

"He's beautiful," she said, smiling and reaching down to pat his head.

"Thank you," I said. "His name is Noah."

"Good name," she said, before glancing up at us with a rather serious expression. "But I have to ask . . . is Noah allowed to sit and sleep on your couch?"

Appreciating her heartening priorities, and relieved she wasn't leading up to a sad dog story, we laughed.

"Are you kidding? Noah owns the couch," John said, with a big smile. "Doesn't even like to share it with us."

"Oh good," the short, impeccably dressed, sixty-something woman said. "That makes me so happy."

Her warm smile was genuine, and after sharing several dog stories, we walked on, glad we'd met such a nice woman. Pleasant encounters are fun, and as in this instance, especially memorable. But we were also happy that Noah enjoyed a home where he wasn't viewed as an annoying, inanimate object—a loving home where he wasn't neglected, abused, or subjected to ill-treatment. I couldn't imagine him stuck in such a lifeless, tragic kind of place, or, for that matter, any cat or dog, but we all know they exist. Likely in the midst of nearly any neighborhood—in my hometown, and yours.

Curious about Noah's assumed breed and various schnauzer colors, I found a reference to platinum silver, but minus a dark beard, he wasn't "that." Salt and pepper, the only description that seemed to fit. Regardless of such trifles, Noah was a handsome and humble guy, and when (or if) it came to finding a puppy to keep Orion company, color didn't matter.

With millions of cats and dogs desperate for good homes, we'd never yearned for one with a certain pedigree; due to fate, we'd met Noah, and had grown to love his spirited, sweet nature. Joyful energy and a sensitive demeanor are irresistible. In an article about them, I read another apt description: "Beneath that baronial bearing, beats the heart of a silly little clown in a spiffy uniform with a devotion to his family that knows no bounds."

The article also included highly accurate adjectives like droll and spunky, noting schnauzer's robust, squared-away bodies and stern expressions that resemble a "bushy-browed ancestor." To that, I'd add: questioning, caring eyes that long to connect with those around them. They seem to love a sense of belonging.

Since rescue societies are excellent places to look for dogs of any kind, I made a quick mental note to explore them. Glancing over at Lola, stretched out on a rug in a patch of morning sun, she looked blissfully unaware of our worries. Another high-energy puppy, her third, might not be easy for her. But seconds later, we realized Orion had switched to high-alert mode. On hind legs, nose squeezed between the fence boards, he'd spotted a cat roaming the neighborhood.

His bark, animated and purposeful, told us that something or someone was very near *his* yard. Barking has a purpose, yet how often do we—dog lovers to casual observers—forget that simple fact? Dogs will be dogs. Dogs *are* dogs, after all.

What is often coined "unnecessary noise," even a considerable nuisance, is, more correctly, a form of animal communication, so we've learned to pay close attention. I remember reading somewhere that dogs are "talking" when they bark or growl or snort (schnauzers often do this when excited or playing hard).

Do you think, if we, the almighty human species, were simply more attentive—less rushed, distracted, self-centered—and responsive, the troubling communication gap that sometimes exists between animals and humans might be bridged?

Always "too busy," priorities abound; but expecting pets to listen and respond, no questions asked, no delays permitted, is a narrow, one-way street that fails to honor their legitimate needs. Not the sort of caring relationship I want to experience with our cats and dogs, anyway. Common sense suggests that most of them are trying to tell us something with their behavior. If we could simply open our minds and hearts a crack, imagine the ideas and useful information that would stream in.

Am I wrong in believing a continual power struggle between our pets, cats and dogs, in particular, and "us" reduces a joyful, mutually beneficial bond to a sadly contrived reality? Senselessly or habitually wielding power over animals (or people) has never been my calling, however. Seems rather pointless.

Isn't it significantly more satisfying and enriching—more uplifting and purposeful—to seek the life-affirming power of understanding? As we know, but sometimes forget, empathizing, yes, even with animals, fosters a deeper rapport, one that nurtures strong, lasting connections. And, honestly, have you ever discovered an effective shortcut?

FINISHING OUR COFFEE, I knew we were pondering the adult cat that wandered in and out of view, as though not quite sure where to go next.

"Wonder if anyone takes care of that poor cat. Looks healthy enough from here, but that's an optimistic guess. I'm glad she doesn't venture into our yard. Not sure what Orion would do if he caught her—unlikely though."

"I see her around quite a bit," John said. "We can call the humane society. They might know how to find out if she's a stray or someone's outdoor cat."

Orion, finally bored, wandered away from the fence and glanced up at us before flying up the deck stairs. He (and Noah) amazed us with their agility. With furry pads barely touching the steps (yet *somehow* never missing one), they had loved to race each other to the door. A game, a form of dog play, whatever their motivation, we never grew tired of watching them sail up the six cedar steps as though airborne and eagerly competing for the lead, while never losing their balance. Neither snow nor rain slowed them down. Ice, maybe a little.

John opened the door, offered Orion the usual treat, and with his coffee refilled, headed downstairs to his home office. Orion right behind him. Within minutes he'd be sound asleep in Noah's old dog bed under John's desk. My office—writing space or writing study (I've never been quite sure what to call it)—was on the main level with an inspiring western landscape of sky-high evergreens.

Lola had a fleece bed near my desk, and when that didn't quite suit her, she'd maneuver her way onto my lap or opt for the beige swivel rocker in the corner of the room. The view, not that she noticed, the window being too high for her, wasn't bad from that chair. Each season featured a slightly different story: nature in flux, birds swooping and nesting (even a stately owl now and then), a pleasing mix of mature and young trees, artistic skyscapes, and in the summer, right outside my window, a mature hydrangea that grew taller and wider almost without notice. Delicate white blooms that turned a dusty pink lasted well into early fall.

Several varieties of prairie grass, tall and short, also dotted the landscape. We'd planted it liberally. A perennial that grows quickly, it swished back and forth like nature's metronome—a natural companion for the persistent Dakota winds.

I'd purchased the swivel rocker for rare keyboard breaks. Not a bad idea, it was a comfortable, quiet place to reflect and daydream, or consider the next chapter in a book or new lines in an emergent poem. I loved the sound of wind jostling our trees, early morning bird song, the occasional rainstorm, or even the eerie silence of snowy days. When warm weather prevailed, glancing out at a jumble of flowers in colorful pots, or watching dogs in a tug-of-war over a favorite squeaky toy, was rejuvenating. Wind chimes, outside my window, were a must—in all seasons.

But regardless of my legitimate interest in the new chair, Lola had something else in mind. Day one, when the chair arrived, she eyed it closely, jumped up and sniffed the cushion, before settling in for a long nap. Must be a good chair, I recall thinking. When our pets show a fondness for furniture, we interpret that as a seal of approval, and we've noticed they can be tough critics. I've yet to spend much time in that lovely chair, however. Price tags still dangle from it; for me, it's Lola's chair.

THE HARROWING QUESTION of a third dog was left lingering in the air that morning. We would pick it up another time, or maybe the desire and mental conflict would quietly subside: a decision, as well, but of a subtler variety. Leery of overthinking all of this—that's when things tend to go awry—I was confident my intuition would point me in the right direction eventually. Logical or otherwise, the risk, the plunge, the throwing all caution to the wind approach, all have their place, and ignoring this powerful truth can spell the difference between a safe, easy, humdrum life, or one lived from the richness of the soul with passion, depth, and meaning.

This vital lesson had come into focus for me some time ago, so I tried to let it guide and grace my life. Meaningful choices, after all, are dearly important. This one was no different. I wanted our decision to feel joyful and certain, not cradled in ambivalence—like something we'd plucked out of a darkened sky to gloss over a painful loss. Our time, thirteen and a half years in all, with Noah never could be replaced, but vacillating for weeks and months wasn't my style, either. I favored a strong sense of direction, and since we are who and what we surround ourselves with, animals included, this was a very important decision. A third dog to love, train, and share time with would be a good thing, right? My heart responded *yes, of course,* but my mind lurched and wavered, insistently asking: Are you absolutely positive? Wasn't Orion the "last dog," anyway?

Four

THE GRAND SCHEME

Most of the people I admire, from family and friends to cherished bright lights in the literary sky, have invested heavily, and wisely, I might add, in the company they keep. Especially when it comes to four-legged companions. Robert Frost, a revered American poet, was among these bright lights, penning this couplet in a famous poem called "Ten Mills" (*A Further Range*, 1936):

> *The Span of Life*
> The old dog barks backwards without getting up.
> I can remember when he was a pup.

I looked for more about Frost after watching the award-winning documentary, *Robert Frost: A Lover's Quarrel with the World,* directed by Shirley Clarke and Robert Hughes. Finalized a short time before his death in January of 1963, the film captured a stooped man of eighty-eight seemingly rich in spirit and reasonably at peace with the intricacies of existence and a poignant personal history.

Frost lost four of his six children. He also lost his beloved wife, Elinor, to cancer. One sharp blow after another, with his son, Carol, committing suicide in 1940. But it wasn't only the film highlights—the genuine, touching way he reminisced about his career, lectures delivered at Amherst and Sarah Lawrence Colleges, receiving the Congressional Gold Medal from President Kennedy—that led me to explore his affection for dogs.

The documentary showed Frost working through his daily routine in his rural Vermont cabin: making instant coffee, sitting by a warm fire, relishing the outdoors and wielding a wheelbarrow while working in his garden. Poets and nature strike me as necessary and proper companions. At one point, though, Frost ventures into his kitchen to boil water; he claps his hands and two small dogs run in behind him. They greet him with plenty of canine enthusiasm, and he bends low to greet them—patting them, talking to them.

"A dog lover," I said to John, as we watched the film. "I knew it!"

Coincidentally, we stumbled across the Frost story in March, only weeks after I'd dived into this book project, so dogs (and cats, of course) were in sharp focus for me.

"Schnauzers, no less," he said, smiling.

"Thought so, too, but we didn't get a good close-up. His dogs, do you think?"

"Maybe," John said, "or someone visiting Frost."

"Seemed pretty fond of him and vice versa," I said, with an appreciative glance at Orion, asleep on the couch near John.

A black-and-white film, just short of an hour, that won an Academy Award for Best Documentary, Features, it's a bit grainy and the precise words are difficult to hear; if compared to the lengthy, highly dramatized biographies of today's hyperactive social media world, admittedly, refreshing.

We see Frost as a man first, a poet, second.

I appreciated the juxtaposition between accomplished works of poetry that have lived on in contrast to the overarching sweetness of a "good life" that Frost seems to know he'll be forced to leave behind before long. Spending twenty-five summers in his rustic Vermont cabin, his love for the area couldn't have been more apparent.

Though I've been unable to determine if Frost had two schnauzers, at the close of the film, after he packs, leaves in a car with an unidentified woman at the wheel, I noticed one or both of the dogs in the front seat by him. A relatively private man—one who wore the poet's robe with natural dignity—Frost, I did learn, as I visited his history, had been especially attached to a Miss Gillie Frost (a black-and-white border collie) in the 1940s. Spotted taking frequent walks near his Cambridge home on Brewster Street, I can only imagine the pleasure—love, comfort, and joy—that this relationship brought them.

EVER SINCE I STARTED WRITING and publishing back in the nineties, I've had a cat or a dog, or cats and dogs, for literary companions. Such unequivocal interest and subtle support beguiles, and, yes, inspires me. For innumerable writers, the plodding work of writing, editing, revising—digging deep for precision, clarity, and truth—is best tackled with trusted friends, the four-legged variety, nearby. The reassuring glance, the wistful gaze (*time for a walk, maybe some fetch*), the wagging tail and attentive ears, and, of course, the rhythmic snoring, all contribute to the creative energy I, like many, value when working.

In my estimation, a warm and inviting space needs plants, candles (especially in the dreary winter months), art that brightens and challenges, photographs, books, natural lighting, and wall colors that spur artistry and channel creative energy. My writing study, painted a meditative shade of blue-green-gray called deep lagoon, is dark enough to project a cave-like feel that soothes, intensifies, and adds warmth. But such a space, one that nurtures and supports the deep dive into worlds yet to be imagined, requires something else: at least one living creature of the sociable, not-too-demanding variety. Fortunately, there is something about offices and quiet work spaces that most pets favor.

The close proximity to "us" is a powerful and obvious draw; but, in my case, I also suspect my observant officemates keep a trained eye on the enticing treats I have on my desk. They *know* those magical bags store crunchy rewards.

Today, for instance, sweet potato and chicken treats (Limited Ingredient Treats for small breed dogs) from Natural Balance, no artificial flavors or colors, are near my printer. Fat content is low, a big plus. Long Dakota winters lead to less exercise and extra weight—for us and for them!

SIDNEY, OUR FIRST WHITE CAT, the one we buried near the daffodils in our St. Louis backyard before we met Lola, was an intriguing sidekick. In typical feline fashion, he was fond of sprawling out on my desk, regardless of space limitations and despite the array of folders, books, stacks of paper, and general clutter. He also loved to curl up in a cardboard box (if way too small, all the better), or maneuver his way, quite persistently, onto my lap. Dark clothing, an unspoken magnet. Sidney's fur, thick and easily disturbed, released plentiful streams of white that swirled in the air and drifted upward like puffs of smoke. After brushing or when he planted himself on my lap for attention, I was careful not to touch his coat and then my face—eyes, in particular. This prevented an allergy flare-up from the notorious cat dander.

I can't imagine believing that all cats, all dogs, are basically the same: Sidney's antics were anything but generic. Personalities abound in the animal kingdom, and the notable or unusual qualities and quirks I've witnessed, regardless of age, arrive *with* the dog or cat. Sidney, for instance, didn't like small children, even though we didn't have any in our home, so when someone wasn't tall enough to suit him, look out. Hissing or batting his paws at youngsters who merely wanted to pick him up or stroke his smooth, unruffled coat wasn't uncommon, unfortunately.

Since Sidney was an outdoor barn kitten before my second-grader, Matt, put him in a cardboard box for the ride home, we could never understand why short teens or children threatened and irritated him. Also still in grade school, Erin, my daughter, must have been tall enough to escape his height radar, because Sidney liked her, too, or maybe he merely made an exception for them because he knew them.

Cats and dogs, regardless of age or history, come with all sorts of curious traits, unexplainable, mysterious, but often fun or endearing.

Sometimes their appearance is unusual.

Sidney's eyes didn't match: one blue, one goldish-green. "Odd eyes" is short for heterochromia, the technical term. Other anomalies are commonly linked to white cats—several colors in an iris, matching blue eyes that suggest deafness—but our eccentric Sidney, as far as we knew, had perfect hearing.

A ringing phone, in fact, could get his attention in a rather surprising way.

WE HAD PACKED UP THE CAR one Friday afternoon, headed south to the Lake of the Ozarks. We lived west of St. Louis then, in Columbia, and the Lake was one of our favorite haunts. Nature, water, worthwhile restaurants, and only two hours south of us, it was ideal for weekend travel. Sidney stayed behind with plenty of food and water, and a friend, another cat-lover, volunteered to check in on him for us.

Despite the independent nature of cats, he seemed to get lonely (miss us?) when we weren't around. *A Happy Truth* isn't predicated on scientific data (books of this nature are already plentiful), because sometimes we really don't need science to tell us what our eyes and hearts plainly see and feel.

When Sidney rushed to greet us at the door—motor humming, i.e., loud purring, enthusiastic vocalizing, rolling around the floor near our feet—his relief (joy?) that we hadn't disappeared forever was hard to miss. Disinterested, never, except when we caught him in a deep sleep, and that could lead to a slight waiting period before he ventured out to greet us. (With age, the deep sleeping intensified, of course.)

Luckily our drive to the Lake was long enough to drift off in thought—ponder the elements of landscape, the subtle shifts in color and feel, a summer sky that looked soft and dreamy with strings of white running through a pale blue backdrop. What a gorgeous and generous palette for the imagination. How can we ever find life dull or mundane with ever-changing color and drama overhead?

We drove across the Missouri—the same river I'd grown up with in central South Dakota—on a familiar bridge into Jefferson City, the state capital, and after a quick stop for coffee, continued our southern trek. Sidney crossed my mind several times.

What was he doing? Where was he perched—he spent copious hours on a rather elaborate cat ladder a friend of John's had made—or snoozing?

Funny how often our cats and dogs cross our minds in a single day. An automatic impulse sometimes, but more deliberately, too, the animals we love are always with us. Honestly, though, I wish there was a better word for the animals we share our lives with—something other than *pets*. A generic label with an impersonal, uncaring ring to it, can't be the best choice, can it?

What about: companions, four-legged family members, fur-babies, dog or cat friends? I see these options on social media sites, in articles and books, and hear them in various conversations. Plenty of us are trying to come up with a term that conveys the trust and love we share with our "pets." Something that captures the actual dignity and importance of the relationship, if you will—the faithful affection they willingly shower on us and vice versa.

ARRIVING AT THE LAKE, the day was mild, sunny, and perfect for the many boats that dotted the glass-like water. A great view was key in this leisurely summer setting, so many of the best resorts, i.e., Lodge of the Four Seasons, Tan-Tar-A, plus hotels and motels of all styles and sizes, capitalized on this.

One of our favorite haunts, the Salty Dog (now, Dog Days), was tucked in a cove with boat ramps and jet ski rental.

Their deck, most any time of day, was a steady hum of people and conversation and, definitely, a relaxing spot to sit on a barstool to enjoy a cold beer, sandwich and fries (health food, right?). Maybe an enticing summer dessert. John and I share a serious sweet tooth.

We love to get in the kitchen, stir up something irresistible. The usual suspects, of course: chocolate chip cookies, cakes and cupcakes, pies and tarts, bread and sweet rolls. But we also like to venture into uncharted waters. A brand new recipe, a fun twist on an old recipe. Anything intriguing with heaps of promise!

So first thing the next morning, we made an easy decision about breakfast. On the Rise, a lovely bakery and bistro, was one place where we opted *not* to focus on calories or self-imposed restrictions. Don't we need a favorite place to happily make reasonable exceptions? If our choice needs some justification, they have a wood-fired brick oven that churns out breads, rolls, and pastries you won't forget. Plus, the brewed coffee and warm, cheerful setting are morning-perfect.

Browsing the enticing baked goods in the display case, a tall employee in a white baker's coat and a chef's hat the color of ripe plums quietly observed us.

Randolph, according to his name tag. Or on second thought, maybe Roger or Rob.

"Need help with anything? Any questions?"

"Looks great, all of it," John said, smiling and glancing up at him.

Customers filtered in behind us.

I caught random comments on the intoxicating aroma, the bright colors and cozy ambiance. A beehive of activity behind the counter must have fueled their animated commentary, their expectations.

I've long been drawn to the solace and inspiration of nature and wide open skies, and morning, for me, anyway, is the best time of day—the earlier the better. So we asked Randolph (Roger or Rob) if we could sit outside.

Handing us menus, he said, "Plenty of seating out there, still early."

Thanking him, we slowly maneuvered our way to the nearest door. Once in the inviting courtyard, we found a small table of decorative black metal. A round, two-seater. A young couple in identical sunglasses glanced up, but hastily returned to their bright blue plates cradling omelets, sweet rolls, fruit. Otherwise, it was all birds and flowers and a light morning breeze. A slice of nirvana, as far as we were concerned.

"Wonder how Sidney is doing?" I asked.

"Probably enjoying a huge nap without us there to disturb him."

I nodded, and we moved on to other topics as hot coffee and cream arrived, along with descriptions of tempting breakfast specials that forced us to agonize over menu selections. Why such an intimidating chasm between healthier selections and the glorious items we yearned to order? Pecan pancakes, maple-glazed cinnamon rolls, chocolate croissants, waffles, sausage, bacon, or hash browns, for instance. Luckily, we'd already decided to throw caution to the wind, as some might put it, so the silly, but familiar, question hovered aimlessly in the air while an animated group filed in and started moving tables together in the far corner.

DRIVING HOME THE FOLLOWING afternoon, we were sleepy, but a few extra stops helped. Overcast, with thickening clouds off to the west, rain looked imminent, and a steady wind blew out of the northwest. We commented on our good timing.

Twenty minutes from home, we could slip in the garage before the storm hit. Traffic, until we hit the city limits, was light—typical for a Sunday. As usual, after a couple of days away, I was looking forward to reconnecting with Sidney.

Pre-cell phone era, I hadn't heard anything from my friend who planned to check on him, but I knew there would be a note waiting for us. Maybe cut flowers from her lush summer garden. What we weren't expecting was the puzzling question she left for us. In fact, her brief note caught us cold: "Why did you two go off and leave your phone dangling by the cord? What if someone needed to leave a message?"

"John," I said, looking at him with a concerned expression, "did we really drive to the Lake with our phone off the hook?"

"Not a chance," he said, laughing. He put down our overnight bags, walked over to scan her note. "What do you suppose happened? How very odd."

"No idea," I said, "but I'll give her a call in a minute."

Sidney was his usual excited self—all smiles and innocence, offering not a single clue. We found ourselves checking windows to see if someone had been in our home. Our search didn't reveal anything, though. Rain began to strike our windows in heavy, wind-driven streams, and just as the phone rang, the answer hit me. A hunch. A realization. An aha moment. Made no sense at all, but Sidney, dear sweet Sidney, was the guilty party.

"Thanks for checking in on Sidney," I said, "but why do you suppose *he* decided to knock the phone off the hook?"

We laughed about my theory, but I'm afraid its thorny truth was borne out in the days ahead. That weekend forward, our phone generated a continual busy signal whenever we left Sidney behind. When we returned, we'd find the receiver dangling aimlessly until I came up with a simple solution: a rubber band wrapped around the entire phone. It worked. His fun was over. But we still had no idea why Sidney was suddenly (this hadn't happened in years prior) so interested in our phone.

Upset because we left him home alone? Bored and needing something to do, or just his way of subtly reminding us how ingenious he could be when left to his own clever devices? Perhaps, he wanted to say hello, tell us he was lonely, or maybe the ringing—the repetitive noise—made him anxious when we weren't home. A mystery with a litany of humorous possibilities.

ROBERT FROST ONCE WROTE a famous poem called "Birches." The last line, "one could do worse than be a swinger of birches," is so matter-of-factly true that it brings a smile to my face. And, in our case, I figured, we could do worse than share our home with a persnickety white cat with dissimilar eyes, who didn't care much for children and was eager to reveal his mischievous side by making our phone inoperable when we were away.

Frost also writes in "Birches" that he'd like to take a break from Earth and then come back and begin again. He's not serious, of course, but only hoping to convey a passing sentiment. Likewise, Sidney probably wanted to take a break from a phone that disturbed his naps. Amusing and crafty, daring and playful.

But that's probably reading too much into behavior that, to us, will always be slightly, and wonderfully, mysterious. A cat is a cat, after all, and most prefer to remain slightly aloof and secretive. Dogs tend to balance the picture, however, with their upfront ways, so I understand why many people love having both around.

I grew up with cats and dogs (usually one of each living indoors with us). John, however, when growing up, had dogs for pets, exclusively, so when we met, he didn't know much about the wonders of a cat. How they add warmth, fun, and adventure to nearly any environment. Not to mention their generous, abiding affection. Sidney didn't seem to mind that John was a novice when it came to the merits of cats, and tolerantly, they got acquainted, even grew friendly and close, until, one day, John realized, with some surprise, that he'd grown into a "cat person" *and* a "dog person."

Between you and me, however, I wasn't terribly surprised.

As theologian, writer, and physician Albert Schweitzer declared: "There are two means of refuge from the misery of life—music and cats." And Charles Dickens, a beloved author, forever timely, had this to say: "What greater gift than the love of a cat."

We were a one-pet, one-cat, household in those days, and naively we assumed this comfortable arrangement would last indefinitely. We *really* should have known better.

Unless you live in an impenetrable bubble on a secret planet, nothing stays the same for too long. Luckily, change is good for the soul, especially when it pushes us to reach beyond confining comfort zones to discover who we are when challenging or fresh opportunities arise. Don't you think that courage is at the heart of welcoming change? That, and a sincere commitment to curiosity, seem to make for persistent, lifelong learners, and nearly always, for wonderful friends, as well.

Pets, noticeably so, often lead the way.

Cats and dogs are wonderfully curious. What is that strange noise? Where did they hide my treats? Which lap is the most comfortable? And what is that loud ringing? Sidney's grand scheme was unforgettable; we have laughed about it for many years, shared this story with countless pet lovers. Here's to you, Sidney. You *are* missed.

Five

STOP SIGNS

It began with Noah. Something about him reminded me of a woolly bear in the wild. His nose, the beard, those furry feet? Or a face, an expression, that looked curiously demure, yet quietly eager? Bears, in photos I've seen, project a confident reserve, and when sleeping, heads lowered, resting on forepaws or tucked flat to the ground between extended legs, resembled Noah catching a quick afternoon nap.

I've only seen one young bear at close range, and though much larger than Noah, I sensed an inexplicable, implausible connection. Like the bear, Noah sauntered across our yard, nose to the ground, taking in every detail, and seemingly oblivious to the bigger stage around him. Not the case, however, because any sudden noise that disturbed his tranquil state—or if he spotted a rabbit, a squirrel, or anyone walking near "his" yard—immediately garnered his full attention.

For whatever reason, we came up with amusing variations on the bear theme: Mr. Bear, N. Bear, None (no, knee), or NoBear (the "no" short for Noah).

Catchy nicknames stick for better or for worse. Plenty surface without warning or conscious thought; some are truly nonsensical, funny or weird sounding. Made-up words get tossed in the creative stew, because, somehow, they, too, help to capture our sentiments about the dog or cat we loved at first sight—or maybe grew to love. Ever wonder how cats and dogs remember their *real* names, yet learn to come to *whatever* we call them—when the voice, the tone, is familiar and trusted? I cringe when impatient caretakers yell for their dogs, yapping commands in anger or with annoyance. Seriously, would *you* cooperate with such an unkind, demanding voice?

Wisely, most of us would run far and fast, or at least stand firm, cautious. Harsh words blasted at people *or* animals in an irritated voice is offensive, and rarely lead to anything resembling cooperation or understanding. Worse yet, when respect and trust are lost, valued relationships with animals and humans are quickly drained of life, leaving behind a flimsy shell of pretense. A painful reality, undoubtedly.

Granted, feeling annoyed under certain circumstances is inherent to the human condition, but we shouldn't expect our highly observant pets to disregard our tone of voice—or our emotional state—when we interact with them. Unrealistic, don't you think? At least half of the relationship equation is our responsibility, yet, that's the part we conveniently tend to downplay or forget.

Interestingly, it's the routine, yet critical, moments that frame the nature—*the quality*—of most human/animal connections. Don't you admire people with genuine regard for their pets—for living creatures? Civilized behavior and reasonableness cultivate the loyalty, the affection, that many animals want to send our way.

In the end, Noah would respond to any silly nickname we drummed up, even if random or puzzling. Humorous ones still get a smile out of us: BooberNu, Scubin (short for Scooby-Doo), and LoveDog. But, Noah, for whatever reason, was gracious and tolerant of human ways. Despite corny nicknames, he sensed our good intentions and indulged our creativity with gentle canine understanding.

GROOMING DAY ROLLED AROUND AGAIN. Part of caring for any schnauzer, we'd quickly grown accustomed to scheduling appointments every five or six weeks. In the car, engine idling, Orion sat beside me in the front seat. Glancing quizzically at me, he readily turned his attention to the world beyond when I opened his window.

Backing out of our driveway, I drove down Orchard to a quiet, historic-looking Main Street. Our groomer was a caring, perceptive professional who loved dogs. Magically, she'd clip Orion's abundant black coat—when long, a mass of thick curls. Even more magically she'd clip his dark nails without going too short.

A good-looking guy in his long and stunning silver eyebrows, a black beard with silver highlights around his nose and down his neckline, Orion, from the start, was none too keen on grooming sessions; but he may have appreciated the car ride even less. Ever watchful (Why are we in the car? Where are we going—to the vet, a nice walk around campus?), Orion could sense when things were, from his perspective, about to go awry. Tirelessly, once he knew we were at the groomer, he'd jump from front to back, back to front, hugging the door on the opposite side of the car from where we stood dangling the most tempting of treats.

Once we'd patiently cajoled him from the car, he immediately planted himself on the ground with every sturdy ounce of body weight (collar and leash of little value). Amazing how only twenty-four pounds of dog can feel like a bag of concrete. Orion must have been sharply aware that there were preferable ways to spend his time. Things independent of water, shampoo, towels, noisy dryers, clippers, scissors, brushes, grooming tables, strange noises, barking dogs, or silly scarves knotted around the neck. The final indignity, right?

Fortunately, Orion endured the dreaded grooming routine without incident, and even grew quite fond of our patient groomer. The admiration was mutual. Steph could calm the most anxious of dogs, loving them, warts and all. I can't fathom the dedication and skill it must take to groom, with such heart and soul, dogs with a host of issues and personality quirks, but I suspect it's a rare ability. I'm sure her four-legged clients are most grateful.

Once Orion was safely inside, my thoughts soon slipped to the hovering third dog question—one that felt inevitable after losing a dog we'd loved, one that toyed with my emotions like an intricate puzzle. Deciding on Orion, our second dog, was fairly easy when Noah was still living; but now, with him gone, it was considerably more difficult to take the leap.

They can't live forever, and one day, the house turns dreadfully quiet. No longer there to greet you in the morning or whenever you walk through the door, footsteps fade, leaving behind a lonely echo. And those soulful brown eyes ... well, you could never forget such comforting eyes, or the countless times an eager wag of the tail, a favorite toy dropped by your feet as a subtle (and irresistible) request to play, somehow lifted your spirits when dark, challenging days prevailed.

With Noah absent could a new, and third, dog avoid endless comparisons, even if mostly unspoken? Would we choose male or female? Which would be best for Orion? How about litter mates? We'd read about the advantages of getting two puppies at once, and though it sounded like a fun adventure, we also knew this option would be a double dose—a serious time commitment.

John and I had deep and abiding emotions linking time and place to Noah. Not only was he our empty-nest dog, our sweet and spirited friend, he also had been a treasured source of support when my son, Matthew, died. While his tragic loss was the focus of *The Silence of Morning: A Memoir of Time Undone,* Noah also shows up in those chapters, along with several stories that include Lola, our second white cat.

Curious, though, is the poem I wrote several years after Matt's loss.

Via poetry, I'd wanted to capture Noah's powerful role in helping me navigate those rocky days: his uplifting spirit, any season, any time of day; the uncanny way his natural instincts modeled the lessons of nature and living with equanimity; his high-energy ways that convinced me to take him for a long walk, even when it was the last thing I felt like doing.

When Noah died in early June of 2015, I reread the lines of that poem many times, realizing how it also pointed to *his* eventual loss. When I'd written it, Noah was a young dog in fine health—his loss was the last thing on my mind—but after he was gone, as I also happened to be searching for a strong and fitting title for my memoir, I read "Without a Care" once more. This time through, however, as my eyes reached the last line, I saw something else: a compelling book title.

Without a Care

Snow arrived early, a fresh
autumn blanket that mocked
summer's bliss, pointed to

winter without hesitation. I
reached for his leash; we set
out on a long walk.

Noah would know the season,
one of life or one of loss, but
... he merely sniffed the air

lifting his bearded schnauzer
face skyward, donning the
silence of morning like a robe.

I'd considered a vast number of possible titles during the seven years it took to write a rather complicated, deeply emotional memoir, but when I read "the silence of morning," I knew my long search had ended. The thundering silence after loss is unmistakable and unforgettable, as many of you reading this also know, and when Noah's last day arrived, another penetrating silence prowled about our home. One of vast emptiness, I'd described it in my memoir as a "cavernous, mocking echo."

Given our history with Noah, we needed time to mourn and honor our time with him. His surprising and rewarding tenure after a gall bladder crisis when he was already nine had seemed like a small miracle. A decision to proceed with emergency surgery, once we understood it was the only option, was not made easily or lightly.

For starters, it was a considerable investment, and as is true for any surgery, there were medical risks. Would he survive, even thrive, for several more years? How would he handle the experience, the recovery period? Monitor stitches closely. No jumping, running, or strenuous activity for at least two weeks. Then there was the unexpected four-hour road trip to Minneapolis in December, in dicey driving conditions to boot, to get him to the Veterinary Medical Center equipped to handle this kind of emergency.

Turning down Main, I wondered if a new dog might also experience such serious health issues. What would another dog be like? What wild surprises, what profound challenges, might we encounter? Insistent questions swirled in my head as I drove on in light morning traffic. I was grateful for the stop sign just ahead.

No action needed right now. Don't even think about a third dog today. Just let the question breathe; a decision will surface in its own time and way for good reasons or no identifiable reason at all. Surrender to the unknown, to uncertainty. Relax.

Since my intuition was freely handing out advice that day—and from experience, I trusted it—I took a deep breath, decided to focus on something else. Orion would be with Steph for a couple of hours, and I wanted to work through a list of errands before then. But, first, I thought about stopping for coffee. Maybe a latte.

Life in a small college town had its advantages: close proximity to everything; a low-key, flexible environment; an array of welcoming coffee shops that were popular with students lugging laptops, heavy backpacks. Competition between coffee shops was a great catalyst for commercial creativity. Some emphasized ambiance. Others didn't bother and relied, instead, on serving the best cappuccino or espresso. For some, enticing bakery treats contributed to carving out a competitive edge.

We'd moved back to my home state of South Dakota from Indianapolis in August of 2008 because of proximity to an aging parent. Landing on the eastern side of the state, we decided on a small town that was home to South Dakota State University and some 13,000 college students. North of Sioux Falls by only forty-five minutes, we were still close to a real airport, medical specialists, innovative restaurants, and a touch of culture. After living for several years in St. Louis and Indianapolis, we valued the benefits of a slightly more urban area.

Glancing around to find a parking place, I grabbed one right in front of the Cottonwood on North Main. Though not a big deal, there are no parking meters in our fair community, which makes us old-fashioned, I suppose, but maybe it's also a good business practice. Encourage people to shop locally, right?

We'd discovered the Cottonwood, a typical college haunt, early on. A welcoming place to study for the next exam, read, rest or reflect, survey papers and magazines in the stack by the door, we liked its casual feel. Upcoming events, lost and found, dogs or cats needing a home, apartments for rent, tutors wanted, books for sale, and so on dotted the ever-changing bulletin board. Artists often displayed their latest paintings and designs, so the coffee-colored walls—beige, dark browns—were rarely boring. Old wooden benches, where students huddled with laptops and smart phones, lined the north wall. Small wooden tables scattered around the bright room were usually occupied; and facing Main were full-length, rarely spotless, glass windows. All in all, an inviting space that smelled like coffee.

Customary temptations, besides lattes with artistic foam designs, usually caught our eye: supersized chocolate chip cookies, blueberry or cherry turnovers, and mixed berry muffins glazed with sugar. Casual menu options—sandwiches, soups, quiche, and daily specials—with prices were displayed on a large chalkboard.

I didn't need to study it long. I knew it well.

After chatting with a young man behind the counter—a tall, tired-looking college student—I ordered a medium latte, a cookie.

I'll put half in the freezer when I get home.

The enormous cookie smelled like the best chocolate chip cookie you've ever stirred up and baked at home; admittedly, it may have been a sugary distraction from the poignant puppy question. Decisions that draw on our emotional energy—that tedious back and forth of delicate pros and cons—inevitably lead to stress and anxiety for most of us. And, good or bad, sometimes an indulgence or two follows.

I know, I know.

Meditation also works. Maybe a nap, a long walk.

But now and then, within reason, it's okay to release the moment—free ourselves from rules, diehard beliefs, or truly stellar intentions. So it seems.

Oh, and by the way, the cookie—the piece I had—was well worth the calorie count. The sky opened, the sun beamed, the trees glistened, and the insistent puppy question dissolved into the gentle whir of a summer morning.

Six

STAR GAZING

When I picked up Orion, affectionately known as O, he was in good spirits with his "great to see you, but let's get out of here" antics. Watching him edge ever closer to the door, it was easy to decipher his canine desires. He looked good. The magical transformation from shaggy and dusty to shiny and well-groomed was one of life's small pleasures. Coat, beard, ears, and eyebrows all expertly trimmed. The silver on his legs brighter than remembered; the festive Fourth of July scarf around his neck gave him a perky, nearly debonair, look.

    The schnauzer leg, tail, face, and ears are referred to as "furnishings," which can sound slightly humorous in the context of a dog, but shaping them properly on a grooming table takes real skill. Savvy groomers know it's best to earn a dog's trust first before going for the traditional schnauzer cut, or any cut, for that matter. From my perspective, it's an art form. Working on a moving target, difficult enough, but the precision needed to trim a beard, nose, eyes, and ears is another matter entirely.

The German word schnauze means snout or whiskered snout, and if you've ever cared for this kind of dog, you know that keeping the long beard neat and tidy is a never-ending challenge. Most everything sticks to it, and convincing your wise and wary schnauzer it should be cleaned, brushed, or trimmed requires patient, sincere convincing. Before the days of Noah, we knew zip about grooming, but we soon learned that within breeds and otherwise—*dogs of all kinds*—their coats are rarely the same and require special techniques to properly trim and care for them.

We loved learning that schnauzers don't shed. Considered hypoallergenic, that's a big plus for keeping related allergies at bay.

"Orion did great today," Steph said, smiling. "Not keen on treats as usual, but that's okay." Orion was leery of treats when coping with any situation he wasn't thrilled about. "Should we go six weeks for his next appointment?" As we talked about the best time to bring him in again, he hovered anxiously near the glass door. Glancing out, I saw that he'd spotted a beautiful collie on a long blue leash.

"With this hot, humid weather," I said, "let's go five."

Steph wrote the date and time on a reminder card, and finally—Orion tugging ever more insistently—we were out the door and the collie went in. After relieving his bladder, we walked to the car, and I opened the back door. Patting my hand on the floorboard, I said, "C'mon, O, in you go." When I didn't remind him where to jump, Orion shot straight for the seat. Rather high in an SUV, he usually made it, but not always, and we've noticed that the schnauzer pride is easily wounded. Once inside and off leash, I gave him some "Little Star" treats made of organic pumpkin.

Noah and Orion loved them. Must have been their satisfying crunch, regardless of the small size. On grooming days or when out for a walk, I kept a few tucked in my pocket. Treats, as we all know, are easily overdone, so we made an effort to use them strategically, but sometimes (we don't need strings attached to everything, do we?), like most animal lovers, we offered treats for no reason at all.

Just because, you might say.

Post-grooming, Orion went for a treat, but not before he looked it over, sniffed it, to make sure it was to his liking. Seemed like he resisted treats when he sensed he was being baited, i.e., vet or grooming appointments. Dogs are super smart that way, aren't they?

Early on, like Noah, nicknames surfaced: O, O-rye, or O-Bear, and when still a puppy, Little O. Rarely fussy, he responded to most anything, but paid special attention to the unadorned "O." Not sure why, but since it worked, we used it frequently.

Driving home, heading east from Main, I tried to remember the litany of names we'd tossed around for O before the right one surfaced. Most were funny, not taken seriously: Moon, Silver, Rufus, Sky, Hanson, Elf, Harold, Newman, Jolly, Seal, Phil, Monk, Blitz, and Henry. As a child, John loved a stuffed toy named "Henry Dog," so I'm still a little surprised we didn't go with Henry, as the steady flow of implausible ideas continued: Buddha, Flipper, Gatsby, Frito, Harvey, Mozart, Chipper, Cosmo.

Time passed, nothing stuck. We liked "Blue," but couldn't settle on it.

We kept pondering and mulling, until one evening, with Orion stretched out, asleep on my lap, something out of the ordinary yet germane came to me—constellations.

Black and silver suggested the night sky, the same colors as Orion. Late January then, it was a bitterly cold night with strong prairie winds rattling bare branches and most anything in its path. I asked John which constellations were prominent in winter.

Walking over to the slider, pushing curtains aside to study the western sky, he said, "Orion for sure, come take a look. Really incredible. No clouds, just stars shattering a sea of black."

"I believe you," I said, not wanting to disturb the unnamed, still resting, puppy on my lap. With furry legs stretched out behind him, head resting on forepaws, our wild little puppy looked content, relaxed. Even his eyes were closed, but I sensed he had one ear closely tuned to our conversation.

"Know anything specific about Orion?" I asked. "Isn't a sword involved?"

For a while, we delved into Greek mythology.

"A great hunter in ancient times," he said. "The three stars in a straight line are his belt, I think. And, yes, he wields a mighty sword. With his two dogs nearby."

"Fits him perfectly, don't you think?"

"I really like it," he said, with a serious smile. "Orion it is."

We hadn't seen this coming (aren't those the best names, anyway?), but we loved it. Unique and fun, and poetically perfect for our star-bright schnauzer, Orion must have sensed our excitement. Head up, no longer drowsy, he looked ready for another round of coaxing Noah to play with him. Or maybe he'd heard a noise: an engine, a car door, the nightly train rattling east through town, a swift cloud sailing across an inky sky, a rabbit scurrying through our yard, a snowflake falling.

We weren't aware of his sharp hearing ability yet; but as we soon realized, when we heard absolutely nothing, Orion would leap to his feet, run to a door, a window, and bark. On his cue, when we looked out to see what had seized his attention *this time,* almost invariably, we spotted something: another dog or cat, a slow-moving car, or someone out for a walk. Something *he* could plainly hear.

Now and then, when extraneous noises pummeled our neighborhood—cursing roofers, growling lawn mowers, kids playing or crying, cars starting and garage doors squealing open or closed—or when pitch-black outside, and we couldn't pinpoint the source of his disquiet, we never doubted Orion's keen radar. Night or day, we knew he'd heard *something.*

John had always loved stargazing. I imagine he would have made a wonderful astronomer. Over the years, in various communities, we've found various telescopes to gaze through. High-powered, and otherwise. But living in South Dakota, where we have the luxury of uninhabited, open spaces, the intrepid night sky is frequently stunning without magnification of any kind. On a clear night, for instance, we can view stars and constellations from our back deck without interference from bright lights or metropolitan, twenty-four-hour business cycles. An overlooked benefit of living in a small, rural state that has managed to stay partially free of mainstream lifestyles and values, I love to encounter an intriguing night sky.

The next morning, coffee in hand, I sat down at my computer and researched the constellation, quickly noticing the abundance of information on Orion.

Cultures around the globe have adapted the mythology surrounding the famous constellation in noteworthy ways.

Seven of Orion's brightest stars form a charming hourglass pattern, and Rigel, Betelgeuse (a red super giant, or supernova, likely to explode in the far-off future), Bellatrix, and Saiph resemble a rectangle in the center of the glittering, twenty-three-star constellation.

Some have suggested that Orion and his dogs (Canis Major, Canis Minor) were sent to the sky to learn humility. The story goes that Orion loved to brag about the many animals he'd killed, but once in the sky, such days were over. Another story, with an unfortunate ending, that accompanies Orion is death from a scorpion. We assumed that "Little O" wouldn't succumb to a venomous sting one day, and the image of the great hunter seemed appropriate. Acutely aware of his surroundings, nothing ever slipped by him—not the slightest sound or movement.

"His [schnauzer] alertness makes him an excellent watch dog," according to the American Miniature Schnauzer Club; in 2017, they ranked 17th in breed popularity. Originating in Germany in 1888, the mini-schnauzer was developed by crossing the standard schnauzer with smaller breeds, i.e., poodle or affenpinscher.

Initially used by farmers for "ratting," they definitely exhibit effective guarding instincts. Other traits associated with schnauzers include: aloof (until someone has been checked out), spunky, quick to learn, devoted, playful, friendly, affectionate. Known for their strong "territorial instinct," this attribute typically reveals itself via barking, not biting. "Highly playful dogs" with a strong "prey drive," stray cats earn their attention, along with squirrels, rabbits, or mice.

If living in the wild, I'm not sure what kind of wildlife these feisty dogs might try to take on. Luckily, our St. Louis cat, Lola, was not hesitant to establish limits with Noah and

Orion. If they drew too close, she hissed or batted her paws. But now and then, I would catch Noah and Lola snuggled up together on the couch, or sleeping side by side in a sunny spot. After sharing the same home for several years, I guess they'd decided to become friends.

WE'D LANDED BACK IN OUR DRIVEWAY. Orion, on the passenger side, was curled up on an old striped blanket. Our dogs were tired, or very relaxed, after most grooming sessions, so I wasn't surprised to see him dozing.

A schnauzer's "deepest need" is to "live as part of the family, going where they go, doing what they do," again, according to AMSC. I imagine one could conclude the same thing about most dogs and cats. They crave our presence when a solid relationship exists. Orion (and Noah, when still with us) clearly preferred our company. Separation wasn't something any of us enjoyed.

I've observed them closely when John is packing for a work trip. As he gathers clothes, laptop, and other essentials, they stay ever close, watchful: ears down, eyes questioning, body posture subdued. And after he's in the car and driving away, they sleep for hours, as if sad or in low spirits.

Time passes, though, and like humans, they rebound. Food, attention, exercise, back in focus. Maybe a long walk. Fetch in the backyard. If it's the dead of winter, fetch in the family room. Sometimes they hang out in my office where they count on affection and warm dog beds; sometimes they simply stare longingly, until I offer a treat. You know the look, right?

As I turned off the car, Orion came to life.

"We're home, O," I said, even though he knew exactly where we were.

We talk to our pets, doesn't everyone?

In caring relationships, they love the sound of our voices; when we are patient and consistent teachers, they learn words quickly.

"Let's go in, O," I said.

As if he knew precisely what I'd said, Orion stood, waited for an open door. After I'd come around to his side and snapped on his leash, I again patted my hand on the floorboard: "Okay, down, O."

In a flash he went from the floorboard to the driveway, and we walked through the garage and out the door that exits to our backyard. A fenced space, I removed his leash and collar and grooming bandana. Glad to be freed of all restrictions, Orion took off, but seconds later, he paused, glanced back at me.

Seemingly satisfied that all was well, he darted off again.

I don't take such moments for granted.

Noah, it seemed, was the dog with nine lives; when the end finally came, it hit us hard, and only a month or so had elapsed since that surreal afternoon in early June when the ending we'd dreaded arrived. Orion was without his friend—the one who, so to speak, showed him the ropes—and so were we. Watching him run around, explore the backyard as if he'd been gone for days, I felt especially grateful for his presence, and the other dogs and cats I'd known during my lifetime.

What if I'd never had an opportunity to know this special, and powerful, kind of relationship? Many believe they don't have time. Some wish to avoid responsibility, but some, sadly, don't value or understand a bond, a connection, that's rooted in an organic kind of caring—in a sense of shared adventure. Extremely difficult to imagine, it's clear to me that we benefit from caring relationships with animals as much, or more, than they do.

Trying times and unexpected challenges come with the territory. Compromises, necessarily, are made to accommodate their needs, funny quirks, health concerns, even as other priorities clamor for our time, attention, and energy. And a puppy, *let's not forget,* is a "project." A kitten, maybe not so much, but that depends on the kitten and personal circumstances.

Still, almost nothing worthwhile comes without a genuine emotional investment; meaningful relationships necessarily take time, faith, and respect to materialize. But many of us also realize that the special bond between us and the animals we love is a unique and special gift. Demanding little, in return, they give abundantly.

How often, for instance, do we overlook quality time with our dogs, our cats, only to be forgiven—no lasting grudges held?

Turning to go inside, a hardy bark from Orion got my attention. *Signs of life.* Dogs aren't stuffed toys meant to stay perfectly still and silent: seen, but not heard. As we seem to conveniently forget, they are fully alive, breathing creatures, and when we expect them to behave otherwise, it can't possibly work.

Also eager to tell us when they are content, uncomfortable, upset, or annoyed, if they happen to behave oddly one day, why not figure out what might have triggered the curious behavior? Explore ideas, consult others, get creative with fun solutions. There are situations, though, when pets simply don't like the people who bought or adopted them (hard on an ego, I suspect); then, it's wise to respect this reality, and for their sake and yours, make a change: find them a new, and happier, home.

In fact, a researcher, Akiko Takaoka of Kyoto University, Japan, reported in a well-respected journal, *Animal Cognition,* that dogs can discern if a human is trustworthy or not. As reported in *Psychology Today,* Takaoka concluded that dogs have a higher "social intelligence" than previously believed.

Dogs, luckily, seem to be wising up to human behavior that is unacceptable in any context. And why wouldn't they get smarter along the way? Evolving during their long history with humans, research indicates that dogs that are misled and lied to learn not to trust and may even find ways to withdraw their cooperation.

I believe it.

URSULA LE GUIN IN "The Lynx" (a piece in her previously mentioned collection of blog posts also published as a book) writes of a lynx that lives in the High Desert Museum in Bend, Oregon. Apparently, someone had tried to domesticate the lynx, but at some point, he was found alone, starving. Rescued and living in a cage, Le Guin describes in vivid detail her first meeting with the stunning animal—how his gaze "goes right through you."

Intrigued, she became a secret admirer, visiting the lynx on several occasions. It's apparent Le Guin cared deeply about the constraints of his lifestyle, and how the animal managed, nonetheless.

Turning to Rainer Maria Rilke, she notes the pure gaze of an animal. Reviewing his work, in particular, "The Eighth Duino Elegy" (1923), I loved his erudite, clearly powerful, impressions about animals and how they perceive the world.

"Animals," he writes in his opening line, "see the unobstructed world with their whole eyes," noting an "openness ... so deep within" their faces, and how they "show what truly IS to us." Masterful, the resonant and timeless voice of Rilke.

Le Guin finishes her piece about the lynx in an equally masterful way. Observing his "aloofness, his aloneness," she points out how this is the very truth of his nature, and how it's unchanged regardless of context. The silent, yet imposing, lynx seems to share something tender and powerful with us: the gift of "indestructible solitude," as she describes it.

Whenever I've studied our cats and dogs while they peer out on the world from a window or otherwise—catching them in a quiet moment when they aren't aware of my presence—I've observed a similar aura, innate, true, and captivating, that points to an inimitable connection to *something* beyond human vision and imagination.

Awe-inspiring, and who among us can emulate that kind of poetic solitude?

Very few, I would wager.

As Rilke suggests: "our eyes, turned back upon themselves, encircle and seek to snare the world, setting traps for freedom."

The comparison he makes is fascinating. Something worthwhile to ponder.

ORION SUDDENLY REALIZED I was still outside, watching him. Looking back at me, he hesitated, a slight question mark in his expression, I said, "It's okay, O. Go ahead, go play." And off he went.

We had a good relationship—understood each other somehow. Not exactly like Noah and I, but in a respectful, loving way. Orion had sensed, from the beginning, the special bond I shared with Noah. But he seemed okay with that, and we'd found our way.

Now he was scanning a skyward evergreen, watching squirrels chase along its mighty branches.

I thought again about situations where humans and animals simply don't mesh. The chemistry is bad, and it's apparent. It's a mistake to think animals don't pick up on such dynamics, isn't it? But besides finding a new home for a pet when an environment isn't working, creative solutions that facilitate bonding can also help.

Incompatible needs and personalities is a phenomenon that pertains to people and animals alike. Are there ways to bridge the gap—what works? Common sense helps, plus close observation and a willingness to make changes. Just letting a dog see that you appreciate her need for regular exercise and attention works wonders.

I've heard that when dogs are constantly crated, rarely allowed to run and play, they can become aggressive and anxious because of pent-up energy.

Of course.

Why not go running with them, play fetch until they're worn out, design some easy jumps for the backyard? Reveal, in other words, affection, instead of a heavy dose of annoyance or, worse yet, indifference. Caring and patience—*when sincere, consistent*—are convincing, and perceptive animals always know the difference.

Instinctually, in other words, they "read us well," don't they?

When it comes to cats, we've also noticed that close and impartial observation can lead to useful insights. What are they communicating in unspoken—maybe subtle—ways? Follow their cues.

ONE DAY, OUT OF THE BLUE, Lola decided to avoid using her litter box, and we knew she wasn't being a "bad cat." Something was wrong. So I watched her closely, followed her around to see if I could solve this mystery.

My curiosity was soon rewarded.

Lola's litter box was in a utility room in the lower level, and to get to it, she had to walk by our covered sump pump. Early spring, the pump was coming back to life after being dormant for the winter months, and luckily, I happened to see her stroll by when it was running. She stopped. Her tail puffed up; she arched her back. And swiftly retreating, Lola ran from the room and back upstairs.

Mystery solved. Afraid of the sump pump.

With her litter box moved to a different room, her usual feline habits resumed. Much like Le Guin's lynx, another example of an animal merely trying to cope in an environment designed for and by humans.

I was a little surprised by my discovery, though, and never would have figured it out without close observation. Funny how little we really know about our own pets sometimes. A humbling moment, no doubt. And a happy ending.

But now, another bark. Orion's grooming session long forgotten, as he roamed the backyard, carefully scanning the world beyond our fence. A dog with a mission, a busy guy, a black sun-magnet.

I wondered, as I walked inside, if he would live as long as Noah.

Longer, perhaps?

I wasn't fond of painful farewells and assumed that Orion—at three plus years—would be with us for, *at least,* eight more. An ending, in other words, I didn't need to envision, or dread, for a long time yet. As I would come to learn, however, I probably would have been better off not to have indulged in such futuristic, hopeful fantasies, as Orion's unique destiny had yet to unfold.

Seven

PUMPKIN BARS

Once Lola, the tiny, yet daring kitten clinging to the screen on my office window, let me pick her up, we became fast friends. Taking her inside, I put her down so she could sniff around; methodically, she explored every inch of our house, as though moving in on the spot. Gently, I asked her if she had a home. No reply. Not even a sly look my direction.

I wasn't sure what to think until she stretched out on our carpet. *Settling in for the long haul.* Then, my visitor, victorious in expression, finally glanced up at me, but not wanting her to get overly comfortable, I had to send her on her way. Hoping to see her again, I also hoped she had a home. We missed our phone-loving Sidney, but a kitten, so soon?

Slowly opening our front door, I wanted to call her over, so guessed at possible names: Lucy and Sally, Tuna and Buttons, Mabel and Lizzy, Lily and Mittens. No reaction, but my silly, random ideas didn't capture her frisky, friendly nature, so I wasn't too surprised. "How about Zoe . . . Socks . . . Ginger?"

Still no glimmer of recognition. Eventually, though, she couldn't resist the open door, so out we went, walking over to our oak tree—crisp leaves of autumn scattered underfoot. Immediately, she spotted them. Watching her chase them—all rusty and golden—for a few feet before she paused and glanced back at me, I wondered if she would make her way to a nearby yard. *Surely one of our neighbors knows where she lives.* She eyed a couple of fat robins, then drifted curbside, before meandering next door to sprawl on the concrete drive for a relaxing cat nap in the warm sun.

Going back inside, I watched her through the glass door, and John emerged from his home office; he'd finally made it through a tedious list of phone calls, was ready for a break. I told him about our frisky visitor. "She may live next door. Take a look." Relieved she'd landed close by, I was also slightly disappointed.

"Very small," he remarked, glancing at me. "Maybe lost or abandoned, but she looks right at home over there."

"Purred nonstop. I had a feeling she wanted to stay."

While we weren't actually looking for a kitten—Sidney's memory, vivid, yet soft, like a late evening breeze in early summer—we knew we would keep our visitor if she didn't have a home. She'd found us. *Somehow,* she'd found us, and that made a difference. Besides, like most kittens, she was playful, cute, and apparently big on purring.

We stood transfixed, watching her awhile longer, and eventually turned back to our work. But as the day wore on and over the next few days, I constantly checked my office window, listened for her sharp claws against the screen. But nothing. No sign of her. She started to feel dreamlike, so on Sunday afternoon we decided to take a nice long walk around the block to see if we might spot her.

Overcast all day, a light drizzle was starting to fall, so we pulled on warm jackets before heading out the door. Watching for the spunky kitten in every yard, we felt sure she'd peek out at us from behind the next shrub. Maybe we'd see her dozing on someone's front porch by a pot of deep red mums. Best case scenario, we'd notice her perched by a window gazing out at us as we walked by "her home."

We saw two adult cats—a dark gray, a golden beige—but not a single kitten; we also saw several dogs, one an older puppy that looked like a German Shepherd, but that was it. We felt surprisingly let down, wondered if this was a helpful clue. Did we want another cat, sooner as opposed to later?

"Guess she's gone back to her home . . . or . . . ."

My voice trailed off, as I chose not to voice my fears about the *other things* that could have happened. Dreadful things like being run over by a careless driver, or attacked by an aggressive raccoon in the wooded areas nearby; perhaps, she'd been crated off by animal control or taken to the humane society when someone reported a lost kitten—a Godsend, depending on the final outcome.

"She's probably in a house we're walking by happily munching on kitten chow," John said, trying to reassure me. "We'll see her again. You know we will. I have a feeling she won't forget you."

Maybe, I thought. *Maybe*. But I didn't feel like talking. Certain I should have put an ad in the paper, or kept her inside our home until I knew where she belonged—hindsight, always so crystal clear, so unequivocal—John picked up on my concern. Glancing at me, convincing blue eyes finding mine, he said, "You did the right thing, you know. I'm sure her family was glad to see her again."

"I suppose," I said, looking up at a darkening sky, wondering if we would get drenched any minute. "If she was ours, I wouldn't want someone to keep her without looking for us."

A helicopter's steady beat whooshed overhead despite the threatening weather. More than likely a medical emergency or someone from Kanas City flying into the St. Louis airport. Lambert International was only about twenty-five minutes east, so jets and choppers combed the skies like streams of cars, trucks, and motorcycles on the interstate.

"We better hurry, it's starting to rain." John grabbed my hand, and we jogged the last few yards to our front door. Both of us were drawn to the tremendous energy of animals: how instrumental they are in reminding humans that life can be less complicated and stressful than modern society suggests. "Made it," he said, quickly closing the door behind us.

"Great timing," I said, peeling off my jacket, reaching for his to hang them in the closet. "But . . . no kitten, no clues," I added, as the same worrisome questions—when will we see her again, or know that she's okay—lingered on.

WE'VE BEEN FORTUNATE TO LIVE in two homes with padded window seats providing a great view of driveways, sidewalks, cars and streets; our cats, our dogs, love them. Whenever we get in the car and leave home, our dogs, in particular, hurry to their comfortable perch to see us off, and whenever we return, they are right there waiting for us. Then, on cue, heads rise, ears perk up, tails wag. With apparent excitement, they eye our every arrival from coveted front row seats before standing and vanishing from sight.

Dashing to the door to greet us with open arms and squeals of delight that sound a lot like happy barking or enthusiastic meowing, dog or cat, either one, it's all good.

Who doesn't appreciate a little love and enthusiasm when returning home? Our pet-friendly window is the first place I look when pulling in the driveway. Infrequently, we catch one of them in a deep sleep; then it's our turn to surprise *them* at the door.

One time, as we pulled in, three heads, almost simultaneously, popped up: Noah, Lola, Orion. They got along reasonably well, so it wasn't *that* surprising, but three mature, well-fed bodies on a ledge only a foot wide was a small feat in and of itself. Yet, two dogs, twenty pounds each, and a hefty cat of twelve or so pounds, found a way. Funny how this routine activity built around pets and a window has evolved into an endearing "family tradition."

A cozy, safe perch does seem like the perfect place to wait, to watch and learn, to nap, and to monitor *everything* happening just beyond the window. From that ledge, our dogs instantly alert us to vehicles, people walking to the door, postal or package deliveries, kids selling cookies or popcorn, neighbors coming and going, random dogs and cats that venture close.

Rarely are we surprised by the doorbell; rarely do we have to wonder if it's friend or foe. Sometimes we hear a friendly, excited bark, but when we detect a wary, more intense tone, we pay special attention. Some surprises, no matter where you live, aren't all that desirable. Kids, adults, or animals wandering through our backyard never slip past our dog's keen vision and territorial instincts; instantly, and eagerly, they tell us when they've seen something unusual.

We try to be good listeners to better understand their communication via various kinds of barking. Differences can be subtle. A brisk, aggressive bark is one thing; a more leisurely bark tells a different story. If I'm downstairs, busy in the kitchen, talking on the phone, indulging in a quick power nap, or absorbed in thought in my study, and a noise or a person gets their attention, I love a heads-up. How they view their surroundings and clue us in is so important.

When loved and appreciated as integral to a family unit, it's my sense that such participation gives pets, dogs, in particular, a special role, a "job," and a unique way to interact with us, and the world around them, that confirms, even elevates, their place in our homes. Could these routine activities also provide a sense of stability?

I COULD BE IN THE minority on this, but why shouldn't we think of our four-legged family members and quality of life as a logical and worthy connection? Living, breathing creatures we bring into our homes deserve as much. Research has been done on such things, I'm sure, but common sense points me in this direction, as well. When I carefully observe a cat or dog (mine, or others in various settings), their behavior and reactions are revealing.

They rarely overlook the little things, either.

Don't they, on a primal level, just like us, prefer a sense of safety, comfort, and well-being? When hot outside our dogs gravitate to shade. A simple, nearly obvious example, but *still,* they clearly know the difference between baking in the heat and more comfortable options. So maybe they are telling us something important here.

Once Noah, during a mid-afternoon walk, strolled up to a tree, and, on the spot, laid down! Because he naturally stayed close, I rarely kept him on a short leash, so he opted for a quick rest in the shade. A young dog of three or so when this happened—and in great health—to this day, we laugh (with great affection) about his ingenuity and quick thinking.

Most animals aren't at all oblivious to the shifting circumstances, the conditions, they live with. The good, the bad, the indifferent: It all registers with them on some level. We've noticed, for instance, how clean blankets rarely slip by them. Cats, in particular, take notice. One of our cats loved to run under our sheets to hide when we changed the bedding; our part of the game, of course, was to entice her to come out. Such efforts were seldom successful. She hunkered down, peeked out at us, like "nope, not budging."

Feline play, a fun way to interact, and more importantly, yet another indication that almost nothing goes unnoticed. Obviously, she kept close track of us, catching every opportunity to play the "sheet game." For the most part, *it was fun,* unless we were pressed for time; then her game was more challenging. Even after the bedding was on, sometimes we'd spot a sizable lump in the bed. Just our cat, still purring, and settling in for a nap.

Sounds basic, but cool, fresh water is something else most pets notice, along with regular meals. I'm pretty sure ours know the time of day better than we do when it comes to food. Like clockwork, they mill around, glance at us as a reminder that "it's time." Exercise and play, along with quiet, cozy moments to connect with them more intently, also enhance their contentment level.

Our pets, like yours, I'm sure, also love a new toy; it's fun to watch them drag it from room to room like a favored friend. And a ride in the car to smell the fresh air, see more of the world, experience the motion of the vehicle, and spend quiet time with us without the usual distractions, like the annoying drone of a television, can facilitate a strong bond. Even brief rides in the family vehicle are a nice break from all things dull and boring. Seeing something new and different is beneficial for many reasons.

Contributing, in other words, to a pet's quality of life, and thereby, ours, isn't a complicated endeavor. Pay close attention. Watch their cues. Stay mindful. Make it a wonderful spiritual practice, as a bonus. Well-cared-for dogs that know they are valued, loved, can even develop impressive manners. Better than some humans, I might add.

Noah, in fact, was a true gentleman.

WHEN WE LIVED IN CARMEL, a lovely, northern suburb of Indianapolis, we had a long flight of carpeted stairs; and when Noah walked ahead of someone who moved very slowly, i.e., someone elderly or injured, someone sad or tired, he would take two slow steps, then pause and wait for the person to catch up before going on. My mother, when visiting, held fast to the railing, while taking each step one at a time. Better for her lungs, knees, and diminished energy level. So she loved Noah's slow pace, remarking how "considerate" he was when she'd made it downstairs to join us for breakfast. Interesting, too, because normally he took the stairs at top speed.

"That Noah," she'd say, "he's a patient guy. Waits for me on the stairs. How does he know I'm old and slow?" A pause. "I wonder why he pays such close attention."

We'd smile, give Noah a treat, some extra affection, and tell him he was a good boy. Praise. Staying positive. Steady, dependable caring they can feel and trust. Never shaming, screaming, striking, kicking, threatening, or neglecting. That's all most dogs—or cats—ever ask of us. Yet, sometimes I see people with a dog on a leash, and am struck by how fiercely they yank them around.

Do they think small heads and necks are indestructible, made of stone? Just five minutes of research reveals the sensitivity of their necks, the considerable danger of harsh collars and jerking dogs around like sacks of flour.

Many have written about such things; many have spoken eloquently about pets and animals and how we value them, or not, within society and societies. I love this, in particular. From the author of *Winnie-the-Pooh*, A.A. Milne: "Some people talk to animals. Not many listen though. That's the problem."

Another author, Tom Regan, considered to be one of the foremost authorities on the treatment of animals, points to humanity's "myopic lens of self-importance" in terms of how some choose to perceive the creatures around them. It's easy to see how this fundamental misperception has fostered a plethora of damaging errors in our collective thinking. Even more unfortunately, entrenched assumptions *aren't* knowledge.

When I approach our house and automatically look toward our front window for that quiet look of recognition that quickly morphs into unedited excitement, I'm most grateful for the magic—the warmth and pleasure and happiness—our dogs and cats have created in our lives. It's humbling, isn't it?

They don't have fancy degrees, big houses, fast cars, cell phones, or speedboats; they can't even speak our names. Yet, without fail, the dogs and cats that come to live with us wield a gentle sort of power over us: teaching us and showing us their generous and forgiving natures despite endless hours of boredom, a lack of care or meager attention, even ill-treatment that is plainly hateful. Most of all, in a subtle way, our pets empower us with their faithful affection and loyalty; yet, we must be smart enough—*aware enough*—to appreciate and value this incredible gift.

The relationships we generate with animals reveal a great deal about us; they illuminate our inner world—to ourselves, to others. Authentic caring can't be faked or staged or sporadic; it's on display, one way or another. This also means our pets, indirectly or directly, usually challenge us to do better, be better, and to earnestly nurture our relationships with them. Caring about quality of life—comfort, safety, a sense of well-being—for our pets can't help but support the ever-powerful equation of love and respect.

Several more days passed with no sign of our curious white kitten. My ten minutes with her felt like an inexplicable occurrence I must have imagined. So I distracted myself by venturing into the kitchen. Baking something indulgent, taking on a new recipe, or preparing a special dinner were favored creative outlets. Almost like a form of meditation when the house was quiet, there was something sublime about the measuring, powerful aromas, the anticipation, and even the poignant memories that bubbled to the surface. Time, it seems, literally stands still when we're fully immersed in doing something we enjoy.

In the mood for comfort food, the usual culprits, however, didn't appeal: grilled cheese, macaroni and cheese, buttermilk biscuits, mashed potatoes, or fried chicken. Cinnamon rolls, brownies, and apple pie qualified as sweetly comforting, but cream puffs (hadn't tackled them in years) and strawberry cheesecake also came to mind. Cookies—oatmeal, chocolate chip, or peanut butter—would do if I couldn't settle on anything else.

Selecting a tattered cookbook from our bookshelves, I flipped through enticing and colorful pages. My random search, I hoped, would yield ideas and inspiration. As

Shakespeare wrote in *The Tempest:* "He is winding the wit of his watch; by and by it will strike."

Lemon bars looked delicious; pumpkin cookies definitely could work. I'd never even had a lemon bar until I was in my forties, but had grown to love their sweet tartness; and pumpkin was an obvious seasonal choice, as "everything pumpkin" had already hit local coffee shops, bakeries, grocery stores. Pumpkin and autumn harvest beers, along with Oktoberfest lagers, and even one called Leaf Pile Ale, lined store shelves as if some kind of fall explosion had occurred. Thinking through the beers we'd seen with autumn-sounding names, I wasn't sure when Leaf Pile Ale made its debut.

We hadn't ventured into liquor stores yet, but with each new season, we liked to stop in, explore all the creative new brews. Label-browsing was entertaining. Blue Moon's Harvest Moon was a favorite. And while the abundance of fall-themed beers felt like a contemporary phenomenon, apparently, Benjamin Franklin had authored a 1771 recipe for pumpkin ale. In terms of historical trivia, fun to know.

According to another article, Franklin also made "spruce beer." Supposedly after tasting the French version (spruce oil for flavor) in Paris, he made his own version using twigs and molasses. But, apparently, the almighty pumpkin was so plentiful in the seventeenth century, it was used any way possible.

Ultimately, a very tough decision was made in favor of pumpkin bars and cream cheese frosting. (I know, if only all of our decisions were this momentous!)

One of John's favorite treats, I'd been converted along the way. He grew up in northern Ohio, near Wooster and Akron, but back then, in South Dakota where I'd grown up, the pumpkin craze hadn't arrived yet. John had relatives in

Circleville, home to the annual Pumpkin Festival, so nearly every year, he'd gone to the event launched in 1903. During the four-day show, the festival website claims that some 23,000 pumpkin pies are sold; pumpkin donuts, at 100,000, fare even better.

The popular October festival includes: Little Miss Pumpkin and Miss Pumpkin Shows, a parade, musical entertainment and, of course, pumpkin-related contests that feature the "largest pumpkin" competition. In 2017, Cecil Weston won with an enormous pumpkin weighing in at 1,701 pounds. Not bad. A quaint town of around 14,000 residents, Circleville had created something lasting, and that's never easy. Imagine the countless family and community traditions spawned by the wild, but homey, pumpkin event.

AFTER MEASURING OUT MY dry ingredients, I sifted them into a pale blue ceramic bowl, then whisked the wet ingredients—eggs, sugar, oil, pumpkin—before adding them to the flour, baking powder, baking soda, salt, cinnamon, ginger. Reaching for a roll of parchment paper in the far reaches of our pantry, I lined my cookie sheet, poured in the batter. With the oven set to 350, the bars would bake for twenty-five minutes, so I started on the frosting.

Powdered sugar, butter, and vanilla all ready to go, I planned to add the cream cheese next. But I needed a half-cup more, which meant a quick trip to the store. Luckily, our neighborhood grocery wasn't far. Overlooking Lake St. Louis, it was small and pleasant with massive windows facing east. So as soon as the bars were out of the oven, I grabbed my purse, got in the car.

About halfway to the wharf—also home to a drug store, dry cleaners, a few business offices, a casual restaurant—it

Pumpkin Bars

struck me that it was one of the nicest fall days we'd had in a while. Gentle sky. Light breeze. Trees ablaze in gold, orange, and red. Marigolds and mums still blooming in gardens or clay pots on porches. No mention of rain. Finally, I thought to open the sun roof in my car to soak up the sun. The little things, like balmy, autumn afternoons, reach out to us like kind words we didn't know we needed to hear.

In and out of the store in five minutes, I decided to stop for gas on my way home. I also wanted to go through the car wash, but the line was too long. Back in our neighborhood, I turned north on Oak Hill, and slowed down to scan yards dotted with fallen leaves. Hoping to spot our mystery kitten, nothing small or white came into view—not until I turned into our driveway, that is.

Our house had been painted a yellow-gold. An orange sun made of clay hung between the front door and living room window. We'd loved the house from the start, hadn't made any significant changes since purchasing it the previous autumn. *Something* so familiar about it, we'd both said.

It's funny how we are drawn to houses that make us feel safe and comfortable. Ours wasn't new. The upstairs carpet, an awful shade of blue, was seriously worn; the walls were dull, painted in outdated colors. Eventually, after hearing strange noises in the attic (ready for this?), we discovered that *squirrels* had taken up residence (if you want to know how we solved this problem, write me a letter!), and the dreary window coverings were mostly hopeless.

But the kitchen was a winner. Standing at the kitchen sink, we enjoyed a lovely northern view of a valley-shaped area with plentiful trees. Our kitchen also came with ample cupboards and counter space in a spacious layout. Stacked decks (one upper, one lower) were equally inviting.

The entire house felt welcoming. You might say it had "good energy."

Lingering on the market for some time before we stumbled across it when out driving around one evening (isn't that how everyone finds a good home?), we took a chance on it, made an offer. Destiny must have been calling, because despite the squirrel issue, the house had panned out.

It's not always the "perfect house" that wins us over. Sometimes it's the house with quiet charm, an inviting window seat, and a rustic, lived-in feel that pulls us closer.

Eight

HANDS OF FATE

I'm not sure why memories of finally finding Lola again are so powerful and vivid; but to this day, after returning from my grocery store errand, pulling in our garage, I can still see the mysterious white kitten lounging on our neighbor's front porch. Megan, a sweet girl—and a teenager then—sat nearby, petting her, and all looked ideal: simply picture-perfect.

Relieved to see that the adventuresome kitten had a home—right next door, as originally suspected—I couldn't wait to learn more about her. I'd talked to Megan several times before, neighborly conversations, and really liked her, so after closing the sun roof, I walked next door to say hello. A leisurely autumn day that reminded me of being a kid again had just gotten better.

"You won't believe," I began, "how happy I am to see that she is *your* kitten."

I leaned down to give the purring kitten a few pats on the head.

"Really, why?" she asked, smiling.

"We've met before," I said, "but only briefly. How long have you had her?"

"She came from a friend's farm," Megan explained, "but our male Siamese, Louie, isn't being very nice, so we let Lola roam around outside and that helps."

A rather loud delivery truck rattled by, and then an older lady out walking her two beagles passed by and waved.

"You're kidding me," I said, before launching into a detailed explanation of the kitten and my screen window and how worried I'd been when she vanished.

"That's so funny," Megan said, laughing. "She's fearless and fun, isn't she? Guess that's why we named her Lola."

"Ah, that totally fits her."

"My mom came up with it."

I couldn't tell if Lola remembered me or not, but before I went home to finish frosting the pumpkin bars, I told Megan that if things didn't work out between Lola and Louie, that we would take her. Never thinking it would happen, I made the offer anyway—just in case their outdoor cat approach didn't pan out quite right.

In the weeks that followed, I spotted Lola out and about visiting other yards, and when we were outside, she would venture over for some attention. Perky, quick, and growing, of course, with our deepening autumn weather, I couldn't help but worry about her living outside. With raccoons in our area, her safety came to mind, as well.

ONE MORNING IN NOVEMBER, Lola showed up in our back yard again. I spotted her from my office window. Stalking something, I went out to see what she was after. As soon as she noticed me, though, she lost interest in her prey, ran over. Swooping her up, I let her come inside again. Do you blame me?

Chilly outside, Lola cuddled up in my lap when I sat back down at my computer. Stroking her soft coat, I studied her markings, listened to the roar of her motor, and realized she was settling in for a long nap.

When should I show her the door?

I didn't want Megan and her family to worry about Lola, but what if she wanted to stay? What if Lola was trying to tell me something?

I went back to my work, let my questions dangle like shiny Christmas ornaments on a tree. Time passed, I got absorbed in the chapter I was writing; but eventually, I heard someone calling for her, so it was time to say good-bye.

"We need to get you back outside, Lola," I whispered. "They're looking for you."

Carrying her upstairs, I opened the front door, set her down on the door step.

"Better go home, Lola. Come back anytime, okay?"

She seemed to sense what I'd said, was even headed in the right direction until a flurry of late autumn leaves—curled and faded—got her attention. Our trees were growing bare, and when she paused to chase the last leaves of the season, I thought about inviting her back in where it was safe, warm. Lola was still small, unusually so, and she looked exposed and vulnerable against the waning colors of fall. With an overcast sky, a strong November breeze, potential threats were easy to conjure up: other cats or stray dogs, harsh weather, wildlife, or cars and trucks racing through streets without paying attention.

I should talk to Megan again; maybe she didn't think I was serious about offering to take Lola if nothing else worked out.

Someone called her name again, and now Lola scampered out of sight; reluctantly, I closed the door. There was a fine line between helping or interfering, watching out for their kitten or being unduly concerned. *She had a good home.* Megan adored her. So I decided to stop worrying.

There were plenty of happy outdoor cats, even though I'd never been a big fan of letting them wander about unprotected from the elements. Years before I met Lola, a cat had been run over in a quiet neighborhood. *Our cat.* Hip surgery followed, and his recovery was long and unpleasant.

"Lucky to have made it at all," the vet had said.

I hoped my new little friend would be spared such a fate.

As soon as John got home, I shared my Lola update. He liked her, too, and wasn't sure if we should offer once more to take her, or if it was better to wait and see what her family decided. Waiting seemed like the wisest course of action. Lola belonged to really nice, caring people; they would know what to do as blissful autumn days grew colder, shorter.

SEVERAL DAYS LATER I PACKED my briefcase, green overnight bag, and early the next morning, tossed everything in my car. Driving west from of St. Louis, I was working with a nonprofit organization in Jefferson City (Missouri's state capital). A ninety-minute drive unless I hit weather or heavy traffic, after making progress on various projects, I drove back home the next evening.

During my commute, I loved to listen to music, but work had been hectic, so I opted for silence. Feeling unusually tired, I was anxious to get off the interstate; impatient drivers oblivious to speed limits were never pleasant. A couple of hours of mindless television *almost* sounded good.

After pulling into Lake St. Louis, a nice suburb on the western edge of a sprawling metropolitan area, I was in our driveway in five minutes. I grabbed our mail, closed the garage door, and John called out from the kitchen, as I walked in, dropped my briefcase.

"Out here," he said, "working on dinner."

But I barely heard him. Something else caught my eye. Something surprising!

Tossing my jacket over the recliner, I looked, blinked, looked again.

There she was: the white kitten named Lola curled up and sleeping on *our* couch. Nestled in a corner with an old blue throw, she looked content, warm, relaxed.

"John," I said, "she's here! What happened?"

There was that dreamlike feeling again, that funny aura of *am I seeing things?*

Smiling, apron on, spatula in hand, he emerged from the kitchen.

"Megan brought her over late this afternoon, asked if we still wanted her. They were also worried about winter, plus things with Louie weren't getting any better."

"You're kidding," I said, still stunned that she was napping on our couch. "Was Megan sad, did she really want to do this?"

"I could tell she was a little sad, sure, but she explained that they knew it was a good decision for both cats. And since she lives next door, I invited her to stop in for a visit whenever she had time."

Lola slept through our conversation, my unabated excitement; but given how peaceful she looked, she must have sensed that she was home. Maybe, with those special feline powers, she knew, in fact, before anyone else. But soon enough an inevitable question, a difficult one, surfaced.

Tossing off shoes, unpacking my bag, I asked myself if I was prepared for this after losing Sidney only three months prior.

Lola was the kitten who'd found us, and we'd never resisted, so going with the flow made sense, didn't it? Besides, Sidney—the snow-white cat with mismatched eyes; the shy, scrawny farm kitten my young son wanted us to take home; the four-legged prankster who pushed the telephone receiver from its hook when we weren't home—would never vanish from my collection of treasured memories.

For some reason, sweet Lola had come along, and undeniably, we'd connected like long-lost friends. *Was it the best timing?* I wasn't sure, but I also knew that Lola was more important than conventional ideas about time. I never let myself believe she would live with us anyway, so tonight, weary from a long day, but still happy, I listened to my intuition and welcomed her wholeheartedly. It didn't matter that we hadn't chosen *her* from a litter of playful kittens, male and female in a swirl of color with an array of personalities. *It just didn't matter.*

I also knew Lola would sense any hesitation we might hope to conceal—cats are eerily perceptive—but, of more significance, perhaps, I didn't want to feel unsure or even slightly indecisive. That would ruin everything. Such a happy occasion, such a lovely surprise—Lola deserved our unabridged commitment.

Doubt can be an ugly trap, and when we land in the quicksand of uncertainty, it's easy to deprive ourselves of the best things in life. Wasting time and energy wishing for something different—something built on the shores of our imagination, on our ancient assumptions—instead of accepting and appreciating what is in our midst and, therefore, possible, is sadly ridiculous, isn't it?

Yet, consciously or otherwise, we all "go there."

"Can't believe she's here," I said, with a deep, slow sigh. "Our lucky day."

John, now setting the table, glanced up and smiled.

Wearing his dark green apron, a Christmas gift from several years ago, he looked like he was having fun. I felt really fortunate to have married someone who wasn't chauvinistic about cooking and kitchens. Stereotypical roles have never been for me, or for him. We each did our own laundry, too, because we went about it differently, and this way, we could stick with our individual preferences.

Forced "sameness" never facilitates a healthy relationship, does it?

Besides, John was more casual about his laundry, while I went with cold water and limited dryer time to prevent shrinkage and wrinkles. In warm weather, I dried my jeans on the deck—easier, often faster—but since he didn't wear jeans much, or think about them like I did, he'd toss his in the dryer and, basically, dry them to death.

Conversely, because I loved blue jeans, *really loved them*, and would wear them every single day if realistic, I didn't want them to shrink. I'd never been a big shopper, not an enthusiastic one for sure, and finding new jeans I liked, even loved, was a rare occurrence, so keeping mine in good shape for as long as possible was a priority.

"Lola's arrival calls for a toast, wine?" John asked, as I reached for a clean towel to dry some dishes he'd just washed. Picking a Pinot Noir—a good choice for most any occasion—he pulled the cork to let it breathe. Admittedly, we didn't know much about good wine. A complicated subject. But like seasonal beers, we were suckers for unique labels, catchy product descriptions, and stories of old family vineyards and traditions that had dodged the weight of time. We didn't drink many whites, used it mostly for cooking, so that, too, simplified our selection process.

"Here's to Lola," John said, "may she spend many happy years with us."

"Cheers," I replied. "A wonderful day, for her and for us."

Minutes later, Lola strolled into the dining room.

"Right at home already," I said, leaning over to pet her as she walked closer.

"Where do you suppose she'll sleep tonight?" John asked.

Sidney slept in several spots, including with us, on the end of the bed; it was also Sidney who liked broccoli, and helped himself to a generous piece of turkey one Thanksgiving. I couldn't wait to find out what tricks, pranks, and games Lola would come up with. Getting to know a dog or a cat is a great adventure, and even though I had no idea what life with Lola would be like, I knew it would be good.

"My guess is she'll sleep wherever she wants to," I said, laughing. I knew us. We wouldn't make her sleep anywhere in particular. Glancing at her, purring under the table, I reminded myself to buy kitten food and toys.

"She'll love our window seat," John said, motioning to it across the room. "Won't take her long to discover it, either."

As though following our conversation, Lola got up, walked over to the window, eyed the ledge closely, then jumped. Continually purring, it was a trait we would grow to love about her. Any time of day, any occasion, any place, Lola purred. Even during visits to our veterinarian, she purred. Maybe she was merely trying to calm her nerves in a foreign setting.

Purring, from what I've gleaned, can mean different things, depending on context and the cat involved.

Watching her notice the window seat in our dining room, for some reason, we started talking about Christmas. Would Lola want to explore the tree, lights, and ornaments? We loved real trees, mostly because of their intoxicating aroma, and Sidney had loved to hide under them, slyly peeking out at us from behind the gifts or thick branches. Likely drawn to the touch of nature, we assumed that hiding or napping under holiday trees was a common feline trait.

Either way, it was a little thing that made the season special. Sidney also loved to chew on curly ribbon, teasing it away from wrapped gifts with ease. We had no idea what Lola would come up with for an encore—what fun, memorable traditions might emerge—but we were eager to find out. I thought of her as the first gift of the season. Early, unexpected, and heartwarming.

If we'd had to make a proactive decision about when—or if—to look for a kitten after Sidney died, things would have evolved differently. Likely enough, we would have delayed a decision, wondering interminably if it was the right time, the right season, the right cat. Fortuitously, fate stepped in, took us by the hand.

Sometimes, when key circumstances merge, good things—*special things*—come to us when we muster the courage not to resist, or swim in doubt for endless hours, months, or even years. Procrastination, in this case, wasn't an option. And Lola, the curious kitten who'd discovered my open window that warm autumn day, had a new home. But I wanted to talk to Megan—invite her to visit soon, and thank her for such a generous gift. It couldn't have been easy to part with Lola. Little did I know we would still be in touch with her some eighteen years later.

Nine

CAUGHT IN REVERIE

Between Lola's arrival in St. Louis and the looming third-dog decision, the steady beat of time had served up many shades of joy and sorrow. But luckily, Lola was still with us, going strong at fourteen-plus, as we muddled through the pros and cons of a new family member—our readiness, in particular, for a puppy. Being honest with oneself is an inherent part of this journey of reckoning, but when I asked myself if I was unreservedly excited about an adorable, cuddly, playful, and plenty-of-extra-work puppy, I wasn't sure I could trust my answer.

I *wanted* to feel ready, *wanted* to feel excited. But was I?

Grappling with a substantial decision means being submerged in a strange and mysterious process. Unpredictable, unwieldy. By default, we hunker down, try to think our way through the murky forest of desires and fears, but this familiar path, no matter how tempting, is not always fruitful.

Frustration sets in as we stew and pace and analyze, and our well-meaning thoughts whir in endless lopsided circles.

When I'm in this position—as I sift and sort through factors known, unknown—I get the curious feeling that *something* more powerful is at play. Determinedly so. Yet, we all know, deep down, that this quirky process is far from an exact science. Emotions, like a mesmerizing ocean tide, yank us one way, then another, so it's easy to assume that using cold-blooded logic is the best, more realistic and sound, path.

Yet, *thinking, thinking, thinking* doesn't always work. Having studied complex organization, organizational decision-making, in particular, as a graduate student in sociology, naturally, I'm intrigued by personal decision-making, as well. Family systems, big and small, blended or otherwise, are just another kind of organization. At the micro or macro level, the complex steps to decision-making mystify most of us, and if a situation carries heavy emotional weight, the inner struggle intensifies.

In my younger, more idealistic and endearingly naive years, I dutifully opened a notebook, drew a long line (after retrieving a ruler from my desk) down the middle of a fresh page and, in giant capital letters at the top, wrote pros and cons. *Then,* I felt organized, thoughtful—less uncertain.

My youthful strategy of winding my way to a decision felt safe and responsible instead of careless and haphazard, as conflicting thoughts tend to feel when bottled up inside without the light of day shining on them. With two neat columns in front of me, my panic moderated, and I believed that, now, the murky details would be exposed and transformed into reasons of merit, or not.

Most importantly, my tried-and-true approach (if not a touch boring, pedantic) felt open and honest, like soul-searching, because as I began listing stuff, I trusted my head and heart—*refused to edit myself*—and dutifully recorded whatever popped into my head, even if it sounded silly or unlikely, dreamy or wishful. In retrospect, my simplistic method—had I realized then that some pros, some cons, were more significant than others, and that a long list of cons, for instance, didn't necessarily outweigh one earthshaking pro, and vice versa—was at least a valiant effort to be true to self. Yet, the subconscious is shy and tricky, an invisible, but powerful and pervasive undercurrent.

As I grew older and decisions became more complex and life-changing, I learned, sometimes the hard way, how the most critical facet of a decision—a pivotal factor offsetting everything else—can reveal itself at the last moment: when a decision, in other words, is imminent. The unavoidable pressure of the process, especially, its final moments, inevitably draws something new and unexpected from me.

Likely from you, as well.

The first time this happened to me, understandably, I was wary. Not to mention shocked that this elegant golden nugget—formerly hidden, yet highly relevant to the question at hand—seemed to unexpectedly materialize out of a crisp morning breeze *after* I was certain I'd come to a decision.

Why wasn't this laser-like insight available to me sooner? Where, and why, had it been hiding? Should I trust its eerie clarity, its apparent accuracy and strength in the whirlwind of the moment?

A curious dynamic that didn't make a drop of sense intellectually, not really; but once I'd experienced this persuasive kind of awareness, I couldn't deny its existence or impact, either. Like a computer silently working in the background, was it really just my soul speaking up at last? A penetrating insight only time could relinquish?

While it felt curious, almost surreptitious, when my conscious efforts to piece things together otherwise ceased—after I'd exhausted all avenues of purposeful thought and exploration—something *new* often emerged.

Could a silly dependence on analysis and thinking dampen, even conceal, our intuitive instincts by blocking a rich inner voice? And when is it wise to go with a gut instinct to avoid the angst and furtive procrastination indecision tends to generate? Couldn't this liberate us from tedious rounds of stress, anxiety, and needless worry?

Such questions filtered through my mind as tempting images of puppies toyed with my emotions. Like a haunting piece of music, the idea itself was starting to settle in, feeling more difficult to shake. And tonight, summer heat having driven us inside, even as the sun dropped low on the horizon, John and Orion dozed in front of the television, while Lola slept on a multi-colored ottoman. We'd placed it near a western window so she could stretch out, soak up the golden rays.

Sometimes I couldn't believe she was *still* with us. When I sailed back in time, imagined her as an intrepid kitten clinging to my window screen, the memories were vivid and warm, like an unforgettable fairy tale. A story I wanted to go on and on. But the trail of history revealed loss, sadness, transitions: beginnings and endings, days suddenly cut short. Yet, there was no escaping such things—no way to hide from time's clever reach.

After Sidney, the charming cat with a mischievous side, perished at thirteen years, Lola and Noah arrived in quick succession. Then Orion, when they were in their senior years. For a time, Lola, Noah, and Orion had joined forces; but after Noah died, Lola, if age was any indication, was next.

During her early years, vets called her a "micro kitty" because she was so petite, but when I looked at her now, the contentment in her expression, I saw a good-sized senior with extra weight around the middle. No longer micro, Lola, aka Lolee, Loler, or Sweet Girl, had matured, blossomed. Such a dear and valued friend, we loved her steady presence and dependable purr—her entertaining antics.

Sometimes, during the night, while she strolled around the house getting water or food, we'd hear a loud meow. Sounding exactly like *oh no oh no,* we had to laugh. The inflection of her vocalization even harmonized with the meaning of the words, and tongue-in-cheek, we wondered *what* was wrong. A funny, human interpretation that didn't really explain her night walks or yowling, cats vocalize and communicate in many ways, and often, quite purposefully.

One thing Lola never liked was other cats (or scampering squirrels) that visited our yard or deck, so maybe something outside was troubling her when she seemed to cry out "oh no" in the night. But I rather doubt it. I should ask our veterinarian or research cat vocabularies in greater depth, but it's okay to leave some questions alone—to simply ride with the mysterious, ever-fascinating currents of the universe.

Lately, though, I'd noticed that Lola slept more soundly, for longer stretches, and sadly, I knew what that meant. Though she'd been remarkably healthy, the wily net of time would one day snatch her from us, and we would be helpless to prevent it.

Reluctantly, drawing my eyes away from her, I rummaged through a catch-all drawer and found a notepad we'd received from the local humane society. Sitting at the kitchen table, pencil in hand, I started to list all the wild and wonderful names I could imagine for a third dog.

Was I testing my readiness, or merely having some fun?

Since many of my days were spent writing books and poetry, words and names were enticing creative tools for me, so I wasn't remotely sure how serious I was in fishing about for names for a puppy that lived only in the recesses of my ambitious imagination. He or she hadn't come into focus in any meaningful way, so how could I dream up viable choices?

Sometimes, though, even abstract notions of questionable merit help us find our way in the dark, and I've long believed in the wisdom of a little reverie to pry open the hidden doors to the imagination. Different than stewing about this and that in a logical, orderly way, reverie is akin to a daydream, a faraway meditation, a relaxed musing—a lovely way to tap into the subconscious. In the end, courting and coaxing elusive, vague ideas from within—cues requiring silence, listening, patience—can spur a rather fickle process. Even if sketchy, almost shadowy, *something* is there—a bridge to a deeper awareness, a gentle nudge, a faint hint. Perhaps, a delicate, yet monumental, insight to finally steer us in a more inspired direction.

Let's see, how about an old family name?

Why shouldn't a puppy have a special link to us, our history?

Ten

HAIR ON FIRE

Approaching our driveway, I immediately spotted Orion. Seconds earlier he was likely dozing on the window seat waiting for us. Flamboyant eyebrows, a four-inch beard, gave Orion a distinguished look: stuffy-old-man-in-disguise appearance. All he lacked was a handsome pipe and a velvet smoking jacket to complete the illusion.

Orion Linus Tobias, his registered name (AKC, American Kennel Club), was a complex guy: Even though we didn't know him well when naming him, intriguing personality contradictions rang true in his name. Linus, of course, was a joyful nod to Charles Schultz and his comic strip, *Peanuts*. Besides being Charlie Brown's best friend, Linus is Lucy van Pelt's younger brother, Rerun's older brother.

The blue security blanket that Linus clings to, holds near his face as if trying to hide from the world while he sucks his thumb, reminded me of Orion's blanket. A blue square of edged cotton, it was part of the "new puppy package" that came with him when John picked him up in Minnesota that bitterly cold day in mid-January. A gift from Donna, a retired horse trainer who also loves and raises schnauzers, Orion's "Linus blanket" seems indestructible; floating around our house, it turns up in dog beds, crates, chairs, couches, and on the window seat. Despite years of laundering and being drug around, tugged on, and slept with, the blue blanket lives on.

First appearing, per Wikipedia, in the endearing comic strip in 1952, Linus is intelligent and wise beyond his youthful appearance. Theologian and philosopher for the comic strip family, he staunchly believes in the Great Pumpkin despite the ridicule and doubts of others. Schultz apparently offered insight into his character by describing Linus as the "house intellectual, bright and well-informed." Adding that such traits may have caused Linus to feel insecure, as evidenced by his blanket and thumb, Schultz also felt the lovable Linus represented his "serious side."

Many of these qualities reminded us of our ever-lively Orion.

Shy, but serious. Insecure, but smart, loyal, and alert. Clingy, yet aloof, reserved. A first-rate watch dog, Orion's canine radar was impeccable. *A dog being a dog.* And contrary to our generally narcissistic culture that seems to want nothing more than to pursue various forms of self-indulgence, that's a good thing.

It's normal for a dog to want to secure his yard, and the people he loves. Within reason, of course. Unless you're famous, notoriously rich, or up to something illegal and unethical and don't want to be caught, no one needs a vicious attack dog poised at the front door for postal carriers, UPS and FedEx drivers, or neighborhood kids promoting a lemonade stand.

But dogs, as a rule, when healthy and attentive, are seldom oblivious to outside activity: strangers coming to the door, loud voices outside, or nearby roofers making a racket. Politely pretending to see or hear nothing is unlikely, and who would want that for a dog, or for themselves, anyway? What joy is there in an artificial existence?

Sometimes we wondered if Orion's first name should have been Linus. Both, for different reasons, fit him so well. Then there was Tobias. We're not sure where that name came from except that we'd briefly considered Toby before settling on Orion. Of English origin, online websites suggest that Tobias means "God is good."

We can't be the only ones who put serious thought into names for the animals we love, but I've never been a big fan of ordinary, overworked names like Rover, Spot, Buddy, Buster, Dolly, Barney, Lassie, Boomer, Rider, Moose, Sugar, Spike, Tiger, Rocky, and so on. Impersonal, generic names seldom inspire or capture the unique qualities of an animal; rarely do they identify what makes them special to us.

Initials also strike me as strangely opaque, since they reveal absolutely nothing intriguing about a pet or the people doing the naming. Might as well opt for a cold-sounding, arbitrary number, and that would be unthinkable.

But, yes, it does depend on *who* is doing the naming.

Children, for instance, come up with some great names. Cute, funny, bizarre, or remarkably perfect. One such name—funny, yet appropriate—that we dreamt up as kids was Puddles. Still in grade school, our family pet then was a miniature "doxie" (dachshund) caught in the throes of house training. During the customary learning curve, and when out of view, as, I'm sure, you've surmised, our cute, squirmy puppy left random "puddles" on the floors in our home.

Few adults, I would wager, would have been clever enough to come up with a better name. Undignified and unrelated to our dog's emerging personality, it was generic in every way, yet, *unique to us,* and the circumstances we'd observed. And we didn't know of any other dogs or cats with such a funny name.

A first, we decided.

So, for us, as kids, the name was special, even magical, despite its simplicity and obvious reference to our puppy's accidents. Besides, it made our friends laugh, as I recall, and we gladly took credit for it. No adults involved—a small feat for any child. Of course, sweet Puddles grew up, was eventually housebroken, and then his name became a fond memory of his puppy days.

Like everything else, those years sailed right by like a strong gust of wind.

During my growing-up years, my family spent a great deal of time with my uncle and his family. My mother's only brother and sibling, Myril drove a dusty pickup, dressed like a cowboy, and lived on an expansive South Dakota ranch with a truly breathtaking view of the Missouri River. He never wore shorts, tennis shoes, and it was rare to see him in anything but worn blue jeans, a western-cut shirt with snap-buttons, scuffed cowboy boots. An old green checkbook stuck out of his shirt pocket.

Never without a dog of some kind—a stray, a sick friend's dog, a scraggly puppy from a busy ranch down the road—and usually with two or three faithfully trailing his energetic steps around the ranch, he named his favorite dog Barker. Silly and obvious, maybe, but an authentic canine name, nonetheless. Since those years, I've heard the name several times; for me, though, it's firmly attached to a mostly black dog (German shepherd mix, perhaps) that my deceased uncle loved.

JOHN PULLED IN OUR GARAGE, turned off the car, and we grabbed our green reusable store bags. We'd finally learned to use smaller bags, so they didn't weigh a ton.

"Gee, I wonder if Orion will be at the door yet," John said, a touch sarcastically. But, of course, we knew he was anxiously waiting there. Tail wagging, body alert, head pitched just so, ears perked to catch the slightest sound. The second I pushed the door ajar, he was in motion. Barking, whining, jumping and dancing in happy circles: hair on fire, as they say.

Greeting us with his unrestrained, "thank-God-you're-finally-home" demeanor, it was impossible not to love our little guy with his sturdy build and determined style. Surely, he hadn't seen us in years, instead of the thirty minutes it took us to visit our local grocery store only blocks away.

Enthusiasm like Orion's was a glorious thing to behold. If one of us felt wrung out after a long, tedious workday, or things hadn't gone particularly well during a dental checkup—maybe, on a more minor scale, a haircut hadn't panned out—his animated, untroubled greeting was a fast cure for disappointment or weariness.

For any die-hard trainers out there, we delved into many training schemes with Orion, thinking that with a little help from us, he might greet us with a touch less gaiety one day. A subdued and forced greeting of the classic human variety wasn't in the cards, however. Never dull or boring, never short on energy or enthusiasm, Orion, to the bitter end, was, like all of us, a grand work-in-progress.

Learning as we go, adapting when possible, and trying to figure out what this funny world wants from us. Besides, what's wrong with unbridled excitement that seems to flow from the dazzling stars beyond, just like his name? We don't have to change everything—force animals to conform to our perception of reality—do we?

Have I mentioned the spirit of an animal yet?

Maybe not directly, or in those terms, but I believe it's only right to protect and respect the spirit of any cat or dog we invite into our home. If, however, you prefer inanimate, "no-trouble-at-all" companions, stuffed animals from a toy store should suffice. While that may sound slightly satirical, it's my impression that if you want a cat or a dog to basically take up space in your home, and nothing more, there's no point in having one. What if someone else would truly care about your pet, provide interaction, exercise, kindness, and even love?

PUTTING GROCERIES AWAY, I asked John if, for him, pet care was mostly a job or a joy. With a laugh, he said he'd have to think about that, so I added, "Off the top of your head, what comes to mind? Honestly."

Orion's intense brown eyes were fixed on us, as if riveted by every utterance.

Glancing at him, John said, "Caring for anything, yard, people, pets, takes time, energy, so it's hard to find an exact word. Sometimes I'd rather watch soccer or read instead of playing with Orion in the backyard or going for a walk when it's twenty below outside, but mostly, I'm really glad when I'm active, not sedentary. Our dogs, our cats, motivate us to get up, and move. Can you imagine life without them?"

I couldn't, and didn't want to, for that matter.

After we made a quick lunch from frig leftovers, we talked briefly about a third dog: the pros and cons. Our rather high standards for pet care—they, too, deserve some quality of life—made our decision considerably more thought-provoking. We knew we asked a lot of ourselves; the commitment was significant, not imaginary.

"Maybe, *just maybe,* I'll call tomorrow to see if any puppies are still available. The ones from the ad I mentioned the other day."

"Never hurts to check into it," he said, with a smile. "I miss Noah, too. And Orion enjoyed his company. I can still see them perched side by side on the window seat."

"Seems too soon, it really does," I said, "but life is a blink, so why wait for months or years to go by? What if there is no right time? Remember Lola's surprise arrival?"

"She just happened, yet everything turned out, even though Sidney hadn't been gone very long," John said, reaching for his water. "We'll never have another Noah, that's something else we should remember. He was smart, easygoing, yet always up for the next walk. And I'll never forget the time I tried to take him out on the water in Lake St. Louis in that tiny sailboat. He was so nervous and uncomfortable as the sailboat bobbed from shore."

"And that lady," I added, "watching you from the shore and hollering out that your dog, being a schnauzer, did *not* like water."

"Noah was a real education," John said, as we laughed about all the things we hadn't yet learned about dogs. Feeling, caught in the snare of Noah memories, our conversation faded, and Orion got in his bed, dozed off.

But then something else came to mind.

"Let's not forget that Noah, at first, was a little wild. Remember how he chased Lola around the house, both still so young, until he mellowed, turned into a happy, relaxed guy. And remember that time he found an apple in my purse, pulled it out, and started nibbling on it?"

"A real health nut," John said, laughing. "And what about the farmer's market, that cool fall morning when he was waiting in the car for us, and we'd left our fresh kale in the back seat before going back for squash and pumpkins. Of course he went exploring, found the kale and shredded it for a little snack!"

We laughed again, but privately, I wondered if I'd follow through. Talking about a puppy was the easy part—and reminiscing about Noah was heartening, surely good for us—but calling about a "new dog" was a big deal. With each step forward, even if tentative, I knew it would be more difficult to retreat, to decide against a fun-loving puppy that would be all too eager to steal our hearts.

Noticing we were lost in thought again, John suggested we get back in the car, drive up to McCrory Gardens—a magnetic place with a multitude of plants, trees, flowers, shrubs, and trails—and take Orion for a long walk.

"Great idea," I said, thinking we could use a diversion that included bird song and sunny flowers. "He'd love that. Besides, aren't the best decisions always made outdoors in the summer?"

We laughed—my comment, in jest, of course. But the weather was idyllic, and we knew Orion would relish time on the nature trail. Of course he caught our mention of a walk, his black stub-tail twitching with excitement, as he waited for us to reach for his collar.

Tail docking, though common for many breeds, finally has been outlawed in some countries, and the AVMA (American

Veterinary Medical Association) frowns on the practice as unnecessary and painful. *Agreed.* Outward appearances and superficial distinctions only, can we please move on to more important things?

We usually walked in our quiet neighborhood. Abundant shade, minor traffic, and we knew where all the other dogs lived. But outings in different places with new smells were special; Orion, and Noah, when still here, loved a change of scenery. Same old walk, same old streets, get painfully tiresome—same four walls, more so. A bored dog is a restless, frustrated animal with pent up energy that needs a safe, reliable outlet. Aren't we the same? So why should we expect biologically energetic animals to tolerate an inactive existence in dismal, insensitive conditions?

Long walks help. Imperfect, though, because a dog is still restrained, unable to run and burn off the energy reserves she, understandably, needs to expend. Large dogs, or small, for that matter, constantly kept captive (tethered, kenneled, fenced) by sedentary or indifferent caretakers is seldom a promising scenario.

Who is more miserable, humans or the dogs?

Many progressive communities maintain safe, well-managed dog parks, but we need better solutions, more choices.

Orion knew where we were the second we turned west into McCrory Gardens. A familiar destination, we loved watching his reaction, seeing his enthusiastic steps beyond the car, the tipped head to sniff the air. Accustomed to walking two dogs, I couldn't help but miss Noah as we took to the path. With his lively step that resembled a jog, a prance, he loved to go exploring—unless it was a hot day and a quick nap under a nearby shade tree had more appeal.

Would a new dog, a puppy, be anything like him, or would such comparisons be futile, even unwise? How would I stop myself from seeing Noah in a third dog, and would that be unpleasant and unfair to a puppy with no awareness of the past? It all seemed uncertain and risky, but I also had come to understand that there was *no time* for fear, hesitation, or endless mental meandering. *Not really.*

When I wrote *Ancients of the Earth: Poems of Time*, I dug deeply into the illusion of time to explore (and expose) how it plays tricks on us, concealing the fundamental reality of the moment. Sadly, when we aren't fully aware of its pervasive power, its inherent mystery, time manages us, not vice versa.

In a poem called "Between Worlds," I described the "pulse of life" as rapid, demanding: an "engine hidden in the recesses of swirling hours."

Sound familiar?

Time, primarily an organizing tool that creates structure and focus in daily lives, can also mushroom unnecessarily in importance; it can camouflage real issues, real needs, and leave us mindlessly staring at clocks or calendars looking for guidance. I wasn't willing to let that happen, unless it was a fully conscious choice.

While time and timing can be dearly relevant, as we'd learned with Lola and Noah, just as often, they are patently irrelevant. Certain of a far deeper story of existence that poetically reveals priorities and values and truth, I knew this was the *sweet spot* for inspired decision-making.

Orion barked at two women walking in the opposite direction. College students, our guess; even in July, they were around—the wheel of time in perpetual motion. Walking on, a squawking blue jay swooped low, and Orion gazed upward—not a care in the world.

In hindsight, I'm glad we couldn't read his future. How quickly, one day, things would burgeon from ordinary to extremely complicated. For now though, following O's lead, we put impending decisions on hold, and focusing on the steadfast beauty and inspiration of nature, simply walked the trail.

Eleven

ZEN OF NOAH

Lola eyed me closely as I flipped on a kitchen light. Still early, but she was up; her animated meow, her thunderous purring, the feline version of "good morning." My reliable inner alarm was set to five, so I seldom snoozed beyond the wee hours, and Lola was all in favor of that. When wanting her food replenished, she was eager to clue me in—night or day, irrespective of clock time.

On rare occasions when I slept in and Lola's food bowl was no longer heaping—a contented kibble grazer until we learned that canned food without gravy was better for her—she meowed with an insistent, relentless urgency. Standing firm on sage green carpet on my side of our bed (from the first, Lola preferred females), she staged her dramatic request for more food *now*. If unbearably early or still deep in the night, I'd put my bare feet on the floor, slowly find my way across the room in the dark, and once my insistent visitor left the room, turn back and close the door to catch a *few* more precious seconds of sleep.

But smart Lola wasn't about to fall for such a silly notion—dull human strategy devoid of merit, creativity, believability—and protested loudly. Sitting tall outside our closed door (we'd seen her go through the same drill with other doors), she'd rapidly thump her front paws on it until she had my undivided attention. A determined drumbeat. Virtually impossible to tune out.

Keep in mind this was a well-fed cat, overweight at that, so we knew she wasn't starving and couldn't help but laugh at her well-orchestrated antics. Not about to be ignored, Lola wasn't remotely concerned with time of day or human sleeping habits. We kept her bowl in a stylish wooden crate, designed to serve as a living room end table, that she could pry open with her paw. That way, our dog or dogs, whichever the case, wouldn't nibble on her kibble (or in cat vernacular, her crunchies).

This morning, after saying a few words to her, petting her, I checked her bowl for a quick wash and refill. Within seconds, Lola hurried in her crate. Listening to her lively crunching, I detected distant rumbles of thunder. I turned on the living room television to catch the weather report. The forecast is almost never right, yet, most of us, for better or for worse, listen to it anyway.

Lola didn't mind summer storms, at least not visibly, but our canine companions were an entirely different story. A dog thing, I guess, because whenever I asked our friends about storms and pets, they all said the same thing. *Our dog shakes, cowers, pants, acts super nervous until the storm passes.* During the night, hiding under the covers is a popular option for dogs that snuggle with family members, but others prefer to retreat to a comfortable safe haven, like a cozy and secure crate.

Some believe this is primarily learned behavior from their surroundings—human interaction, per se. Storm anxiety passed on to our pets. I'm not sure that John and I have much storm anxiety, however. Yet, our dogs reliably exhibit this trait as they mature, becoming increasingly aware of common planetary realities, i.e., storms.

So maybe we do, even if imperceptible.

As fun-loving, happily oblivious puppies, Noah and Orion were largely unaware of weather conditions, but as they experienced the world around them—tuned in ever more closely to their environment—gradually, they began to notice everything. And much like watching a young child grow and develop, they soon figured out that thunder, strong winds, and heavy rain were undesirable and anxiety-provoking; so regardless of cause—human influence, or otherwise—we are sensitive to their fear and discomfort.

This morning, hearing nothing severe in the forecast, I meandered back into the kitchen, as Lola emerged from her crate. Purring, of course.

One of my favorite authors, Eckhart Tolle, once humorously noted: "I have lived with several Zen masters—all of them cats."

He makes a good point.

Lola, in fact, would be a good Zen master: rise early, greet the day, seek the sun, nap often. Watching her stretch out to catch the morning sun—soaking up warm, soothing rays—or perch near a window to observe nature and the world beyond, her deeply relaxed, almost meditative, state often reminds me to cultivate tranquility: sink into silence whenever possible, rest frequently (even if briefly), and worry less about past and future—on a minor scale, the ever-changing, usually wrong forecast. Whenever I spotted Lola sleeping,

I said to myself: *no worries*. Like nature, animals guide and teach us in profound, lifesaving ways.

Émile Zola, novelist, playwright, journalist, told us: "The fate of animals is of greater importance to me than the fear of appearing ridiculous; it is indissolubly connected with the fate of men." Of this, I have no doubt.

WE LIKED TO GRIND FRESH coffee beans in the morning; we'd also switched to a Chemex with a permanent filter. Like most, we'd owned a multitude of coffeemakers, but we wanted to simplify, and no longer felt good about electric coffeemakers with hidden parts and pieces that couldn't be seen or cleaned. So the one-piece glass option with no internal parts to fuss over found its way into our kitchen.

Invented in 1941 by chemist Dr. Peter Schlumbohm, he liked to improve objects used by many on a regular basis by enhancing product appearance or functionality.

The smooth, seamless hourglass design of the Chemex, crafted from a single piece of borosilicate glass, has survived a waterfall of coffee trends and fads.

No small feat.

A powerful example of creative genius, the Schlumbohm coffeemaker bridged two distinct orientations—science, art and design—to envision a useful product that was *new* in a vigorous industry originating in the fifteenth century. The history of coffee, like most subjects plucked out of long ago, is hardly definitive. But regardless of time's impact, coffee is an extremely valuable commodity: Only oil surpasses the ongoing popularity of coffee beans in terms of legally traded commodities.

Listening to the whirr of the grinder, I turned on the electric water kettle, and went to catch a headline or two on the morning news. Predictable, repetitive, with an emphasis on violence and discord, as soon as I heard the water boiling, I clicked off the power button on the remote, and glanced out the eastern window just as the sky morphed into delicate shades of pink, yellow, and orange. A magic show in its own right. No headlines needed.

CERTAIN I WOULD FOLLOW THROUGH on that call about the puppies, something about the drenching rain that arrived later that morning gave me pause. Bright, sunny days empower us, don't they? I named my website and author blog *Sunny Room Studio* for that very reason. Who doesn't need a warm, inviting place—a sunny room?

If unavailable in the physical realm, why not create such a place via the warmth of words, ideas, and friendship? We can value any kind of space (real or virtual) that provides a viable escape from the mundane, the tragic, the confusion and chaos that swirls endlessly on the national scene—and most assuredly within family systems, organizations of all kinds, neighborhoods, communities, schools and colleges, places of employment, political and religious systems.

Yellow, however, connotes more than sunny days or light-filled rooms. Vincent Van Gogh captured how it can impact our feelings even in the abstract sense, with this: "I think that I still have it in my heart someday to paint a bookshop with the front yellow and pink in the evening . . . like a light in the midst of the darkness."

I can imagine such an inviting place, can't you?

The puppy call awaited my attention, but I stalled—I wasn't a big phone person after all—and sat down at my computer instead to log in to my website. Launched in early 2010, I loved its upbeat, introspective slant: how it had gradually evolved into a steady, refreshing source of inspiration. With rare exception, we have to be our own answers, *our own field of heightened awareness*. And in my "sunny room," my writing studio in cyberspace, I'd found the perfect place to delve into spiritual and literary topics, frequently tapping my sociology background to explore societal and cultural issues inherent to the marvelous, yet troubling, human condition.

That year, late November, I'd penned one of my most popular blog posts: "The Zen of Noah." Weaving in expressive dog photographs, readers loved the tenor, the overall message, of the post. I recall thinking it should be developed into a book someday. Assuming Noah's wise inner voice, unwittingly I'd tapped a rich vein: a powerful co-mingling of humor and truth that resonated for many reasons.

When I posted "The Zen of Noah," he was going strong, and I'd explained that our little dog of eight years appeared to experience the world around him with a peaceful heart. Surely, I mused, Noah had unspoken wisdom to share; surely, it was right to honor his lively spirit, his apparent contentment.

Granted, I couldn't read a private canine mind; but after a longish relationship with Noah—observing him closely, studying his behavior—I'd noted his reaction to environmental conditions and various stimuli, watched him cope with change and surprise, seen him excited, low-energy, and alert, so I had an idea (educated guess?) what he might choose to articulate, if possible.

Some of Noah's advice was offered, more or less, in jest. Unsurprisingly, though, pearls of wisdom, primarily tongue-in-cheek (a phrase, an idiom, dating back to the early 1800s) may have a greater influence on us than formal ripples of advice that flow in our direction. Most of us are less resistant to information that simply lands in our hearts with a mighty "ring of truth." Ideas and insights that don't hit us over the head, in other words, appear to reach us on a deeper level, because we're more receptive to information that seeps in casually, comfortably—almost, imperceptibly.

As I continued to ponder the call I planned to make, I searched for the post. And when I read "The Zen of Noah" again, his memory grew strong and vivid, as if he were here with us once more—napping on the window seat, asleep near my feet, or waiting for a treat. Sensing that I hadn't surrendered—not in the deep emotional sense—to his absence, and even though I had no intention of relinquishing my memories as "part of the past," and thus, "less important than today," I also wasn't positive I'd spent enough time simply *being* with his memory.

Uncertainty, indecision hung thick in the air, like another menacing storm cloud set to erupt. But as his faithful ghost writer, once I'd reflected on his keen insights, I felt calmer, almost refreshed, and slightly more empowered to forge ahead. Firmly, I told myself that a single phone call requesting basic information was *not* a formal commitment. Merely a safe, exploratory, why-not-learn-more step.

To set the tone, the mood, of the Noah piece, I'd incorporated Zen-type quotes.

> Knock on the sky and listen to the sound!
> —Zen saying

> Zen is a kind of unlearning. It teaches you how to drop that which you have learned, how to become unskilled again, how to become a child again.... —Osho

All conditioned things are impermanent.
Work out your own salvation with diligence.
—Buddha's last words

But Zen, for me, was a powerful, life-enhancing simplification of contemporary lifestyles that draw too much from too many, forcing people into restrictive boxes nearly impossible to extricate themselves from. It also points to a pressing societal and cultural need: to tap into a deeper perspective. It's one way a sweltering stream of daily drama can be sidelined, if not avoided. We make much better choices when we are centered, less distracted by all the "crazy noise" circulating around us.

So in our gentle dog's enduring memory, here are his witty and wise suggestions, with minor edits, as initially shared in "The Zen of Noah."

- Wear something warm in the winter if only to humor others.
- Play in the snow even when it's cold.
- Practice patience with humans.
- Stay near the kitchen during the holidays.
- Nap in sunlight . . . always appreciating a sunny room.
- Stick with carrots for a treat.
- Go for a walk once a day, twice is better.
- Find friends to play with, share your toys.
- When bored, chase squirrels, but do no harm.
- Sleep in on cold snowy days or daydream a bit.
- Enjoy nature in stillness.
- When someone takes your picture, grin and bear it.
- Forget ego; it's a silly kind of nonsense, and only for the big dogs.

- When feeling blue, stare up at the sky.
- Yoga mats are great places for morning naps.
- If the cat eats your food, accept what is.
- Run free when your collar is off.
- Show excitement when visitors knock at your door.
- Bark at people walking through your yard to greet them properly.
- Don't bite children or adults.
- When a bath is necessary, stay calm.
- Chew on your Christmas gifts, but mutter a quick thank you first.
- Learn to play fetch.
- Remember, ice water from Starbucks is better.
- Investigate life, remain curious.
- Trips to the vet are sometimes unpleasant and also frightening, but show gratitude anyway.
- When potato chips are offered, one is okay.
- If you get a new collar, wear it proudly.
- Shun trips outside in the black of night.
- Sleep under Christmas trees.
- If the cat stares up at you, stay humble.
- A little snow won't bother furry paws.
- Reflect on the day with a peaceful heart.

There is something uplifting—casual and friendly, not pretentious or stuffy—in Noah's humble tidbits of wisdom. My favorite one: Sleep under Christmas trees. Cats napping under holiday trees were one thing, but not to be outdone, Noah and Orion also liked to doze on fluffy Christmas tree skirts, as if celebrating the season in their own way.

By now, Noah had come into sharp focus for me again.

Eyes that consoled. A content demeanor. Never rude, demanding, or impatient. Always ready for a nap, a walk, a ride in the car, or a treat.

He loved to spend time with us in the kitchen, resting on a rug while we worked on dinner, a birthday cake, bacon and eggs for breakfast. Oatmeal with small pieces of apple was a favorite treat, and when we chopped or diced on the cutting board, he seemed to know when it was something he liked.

EARLY AFTERNOON CAME and went. The sky cleared. I glanced at the clock once more, as though seeking guidance. A clue, a sign, that *this* was indeed the "right time" to call. There was no deadline, of course: only the chance that all the puppies would be sold. Hoping that wasn't the case, I pulled out my notes, reached for my cell phone. I was making a mountain out of a molehill, as the timeless saying goes, and creating needless anxiety around a routine task.

But impulsivity has never been my forte, or my desire. Caught in such a sticky web, aren't we at the mercy of our latest whim? And this was a long-term decision, of that I was certain. A puppy grows fast, and one day, you wake up to a young dog, an aging dog, and finally, one very senior dog with a painful limp, worrisome skin bumps, and any number of life-threatening ailments.

The pet path—no matter how eager we are to assume its dangers, joys, or special challenges—is rarely without surprise. The worst happens; the best happens. Even caring deeply can feel extremely stressful when things go awry.

Yet, the good days show up as well, and we find ourselves in a happy, contented space, wondering how we would live without them. Until one day, a day like all the others, we wake up, realize that life with our beloved cat or dog feels tenuous, and we ask ourselves how soon the dreadful end will arrive.

Love is like that, isn't it? Rewarding and unbearable, all at the same time. But I looked outside. The summer sun radiated courage and life. I knew it was time.

"Hi," I said, in a hopeful tone, before getting right to the point. "We noticed you are selling schnauzer puppies. Any still available?" Pausing, I added, "Just curious. We're not in any hurry."

Why was I hedging?

Maybe I hoped to convey my fuzzy feelings—vacillating thoughts generated by overthinking—or at the other end of the spectrum, I might have been protecting myself from a polite, "I'm sorry, they're all sold."

At the heart of the matter, though, was my earnest wish to connect with a puppy to follow in Noah's Zen-like footsteps (be sure to catch the *Zen of Noah Recap* at the end of the book). If one possessed such promise, I knew I would pick up on it. If not, I would sense that, too.

Our first meeting, *should there be one,* would reveal all.

Part Two
EVERYTHING TO GAIN

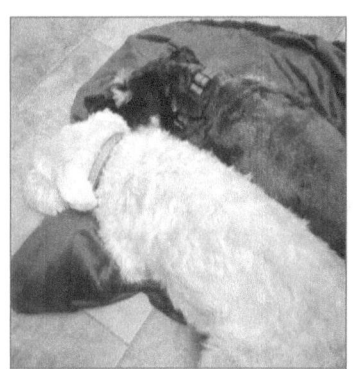

Hannah and Orion   **Hannah**

The greatness of a nation and its moral progress can be judged by the way its animals are treated.
—MAHATMA GANDHI

Twelve

DEEP-TONED BELL

We have a small, but lovely, rock garden in our backyard. Three feet in diameter, it sits off by itself. When we collected rocks, placed them just so, it was cradled between two massive trees in a quiet, shady spot. But the trees—honey locust and evergreen—were later lost in the turbulence of a summer storm, so now the rock garden sits in a bright, sunny spot between two young trees: Royal Frost birch, Sienna Glen maple. Yet shade-loving perennials don't do well in sun, so last spring I took up the plants that were struggling, moved them to a better location, and set down varieties that thrive in more sunlight.

Surprisingly, an asparagus fern really took off. Not a perennial in our area, but I've always loved their airiness, their whimsical qualities. I'd hoped to transplant it, bring it inside for winter, but a killing frost arrived sooner than we expected. When spring rolls around, I'll probably plant another one. They favor some shade, as well, and now

Noah's garden, as we call it, has an inspiring balance of sun and shade.

When I called our veterinarian that deceptively bright day in early June, I had to force myself to speak. "I don't think Noah is going to make it." Hard words to shake loose. And right away, I wanted to take them back, imagine that things weren't so dire. But he couldn't keep his food down, was sad and worn out. We'd focused closely on dietary issues since his gall bladder surgery in late 2010. Low-fat options all the way. Now, though, in 2015, Noah's kidneys were failing; lab work had confirmed our fears, and given his senior status, we'd exhausted viable intervention options. Yet, it all felt surreal—a day I'd imagined without complete comprehension.

The night before we'd been outside enjoying the cool evening air, watching Noah and Orion meander around the backyard. I took several pictures of them that night. There was something so peaceful about their interaction. Noah stretched out in the grass: relaxing, soaking up the smells of spring. His gaze, free of angst, free of fear or pain, and I'd wondered, yet again, how we would manage without him.

Many excellent articles and books have been written about grief after losing a beloved pet. Yet another intense seismic wave in the fabric of life, some may try to minimize a pet's death with foolish words like "just a dog" or "just a cat," but as we trek through our days, we slowly build lasting bonds with the animals under our roof. A connection that grows deep and strong. A friendship based on loyalty, trust, and learning together.

As I worked on this book, I ran across a 2017 article by a professor of psychology at Knox College, Frank T. McAndrew. The headline alone was good reason to read on: "Why Losing a Dog Can Be Harder Than Losing a Relative or Friend."

I'm not sure we really need to compare which kind of loss is more difficult than the next, but McAndrew, an "evolutionary social psychologist," an "award-winning teacher," and frequent contributor to many notable media outlets, sets the record straight in a cogent, helpful way. Mourning the loss of a pet is *not* an overreaction.

I found his article in "The Conversation," known for "academic rigor, journalistic flair." I wonder, though, why we still feel the need for approval to grieve the death of a cat or a dog—any animal for that matter—that we loved and cared for exactly like a valued member of our own family?

Unfortunately, our "advanced society" with its complexities and myriad issues, hasn't done a great job when it comes to understanding the riveting dynamics of grief, or permitting people to contend with loss (pets and/or humans) in ways that honor the painful cessation of deeply meaningful relationships. I wrote at length about this topic in my memoir about my son's death, at twenty-seven, from suicide and addiction. Living through that experience, I immediately sensed an alarming insensitivity to the heavy emotional demands of sudden absence.

Generally speaking, some people acted like a few days should do it. Impossible. Hardly a common cold, a seasonal flu, loss, in many ways, *is* the human condition, and as humans, we all know pain. And deep sadness. The kind that literally flattens us. I hope, as we evolve, we'll begin to lean more heavily on our intuition—trusting and following our inner wisdom, instead of dancing around cultural expectations.

Generic rules and convenient assumptions surrounding loss don't apply. Every loss is deeply personal.

With Noah at my side, the world felt more complete and certain, even more worthwhile. I missed his presence deeply:

a shared history, our daily routine, the way he could grasp feeble human efforts to communicate. I'd never hesitated to speak to him, or Orion, in complete sentences and was frequently amazed at how they could pick up on content and context.

Along these lines, this article was intriguing: "People Who Talk to Their Pets Are Actually Smarter Than Those Who Don't." I gleaned from this, and similar articles, that they are referring to a form of social intelligence, and that anthropomorphizing is attributing "human traits, emotions, or intentions to non-human entities."

Viewed as our brains at work—tapping creative tendencies, adapting, and fully recognizing life in its many forms—on a common sense level, if we don't talk to our pets, how can we respect and understand their intelligence, or help them learn the plentiful oddities of human behavior?

I say "excuse me" to our dogs, and reliably, they quickly move aside. Whether it's tone, words, or merely sensing what I want them to do, they respond in surprisingly perceptive ways. I'm sure there are situations where people resort to kicking a dog when underfoot, or otherwise in the way. Why would anyone inflict unnecessary pain on an animal when a simple "excuse me" or "excuse please" works just fine? They aren't doormats, after all.

I've also read (Scott Greenstone, *Seattle Times*) that many homeless people take better care of their pets than of themselves. Even if they have trouble getting into shelters with a pet, homeless people with pets (reportedly 5 to 10 percent) try to find ways to care for their animals. Progressive cities are making it easier. Doney Memorial Pet Clinic (named for Bud Doney, a veterinarian who launched the clinic in 1985) in downtown Seattle is fully funded by donations; volunteers estimate seeing a thousand clients a year. Clearly, we need more options like this.

Fortunately, we are able to take care of our pets, but not everyone is in a position to adequately maintain the magical creatures so willing to befriend humans. And, regrettably, as we all know, some people don't worry much about their animals or seek quality care for them when needed. A painful reality to acknowledge, isn't it?

OUR FINAL GOOD-BYE TO Noah left behind a trail of tears, but love is like that, and spirited journeys of the heart tend to reveal their true depth and meaning when loss arrives. Countless gifts left in their wake shine on, though. One thing we've appreciated about living with dogs and cats is how frequently they remind us not to take life, or ourselves, too seriously. A red ball or favorite toy tucked in a mouth and handed off to us, for instance, is an instant reminder to lighten up, play some, take a break, because life *really* is short.

We know this is true, yet, sometimes we fall into a frightening trap: We live like there will always be another time, a better time.

Quite possibly, though, a "better time" doesn't roll around. Our days, their days, are *always* numbered. Putting off things, especially seemingly smaller, not quite so important things, until the "perfect moment" arrives is invariably a step down the dark, dreary path of regret: a destiny most hope to avoid. But if we don't live with awareness (eyes, hearts, and minds open) and mindful (conscious) intention—with values and well-considered priorities front and center—it happens a lot. I've been there, haven't you?

Dogs and cats, however, experience time differently. Fully "here," their steady presence is independent of the wicked game of time, and what a gift to humankind. As we know from experience, humans are habitually distracted—if not emotionally and mentally lost—by worry, impatience, frustration, work and career competition, the shifting or overwhelming demands of each day, an array of inevitable setbacks and problems, the rapid pace of change (expected or otherwise), and, of course, the vicious struggle to "get somewhere" fast. Somewhere else, most likely.

I loved special moments when Noah's hypnotic gaze was enough to pull me away from less-than-critical activities, to-do lists, or senseless TV gazing. As our first "no worries" dog, frequently I caught him resting quietly near windows or glass doors, seemingly soaking up the moment. Noah's view of the world spoke volumes about the shortsighted nature of our insistent busyness. Like the sound of a deep-toned bell penetrating the eerie shadows of existence, the sharp contrast between clumsy human habits and Noah's endearing presence was unmistakable.

Of course an inclination to notice and appreciate revealing realities is necessary. If I hadn't been eager to *learn* from our four-legged family members, clearly, I would have overlooked priceless insights. Inspiration is everywhere—most sources, free—but putting aside ego and flimsy assumptions is integral to this powerful equation.

Missing Noah meant all of this, and much more. I knew a puppy would bring an entirely different kind of energy into our home—a playful, determined exuberance in a toy-based world with a fierce desire to chew on *everything*. Gentle handholding and help learning many things, like noisy vacuums aren't the enemy, would be in order. Noah never believed us on that one, though.

Quickly heading to the nearest door and refusing to come in until the vacuum was off and out of sight, he held firm whenever we dared to clean our rugs.

Now, though, a kind voice was explaining that her puppies were all gone, but she went on to add that her sister would have a litter of white schnauzers in the weeks ahead. I took a deep breath. Noah's salt-and-pepper coat came to mind. *White. That might resemble him a bit.*

Jotting down her sister's name and phone number, I felt secretly lucky. I'd been granted a slight reprieve. I could kick back, go on mulling things around, or opt for a total change of heart. Welcome relief swept over me, as Orion ambled to the slider, barked, and glanced back at me as if to say, "So what's the delay here?"

I was reminded of a heartening book of poetry by John Yamrus. Consisting of twenty-three poems, the first one in *BARK* is "My Dogs." It rings true, makes me smile. Essentially, he lists the *many* things his dogs like to bark at—his neighbors, the UPS man, the vacuum cleaner—before wrapping things up with a poetic touch of humor: If not barking, they're just waiting for something to bark at.

Finally, he points out that they are "good dogs."

Orion was a good dog, too. His personality was his own, though. More shy than Noah, yet, more eager and excitable, Orion had a surprisingly gentle, loving streak, one he shared on a very discriminating basis. To those who didn't know him, he may have seemed loud, edgy, and somewhat rambunctious. Orion's typical bark, like any good watch dog, was certain and convincing. Maybe a touch intimidating.

Walking over to the door, cell phone still in hand, I pulled it open, watched him run across the deck, practically sailing over the steps. Waiting for a bark, we joked that there was always *something* outside for Orion to comment on.

Like the distant constellation, O had a most endearing sparkle, a unique type of charm. So how would our little guy do with a puppy? Too rough, too bossy? Or would he readily convert to friend, teacher, leader, and playmate—enjoying the antics and companionship of a cute, bouncy puppy?

Drastically different than his three-plus years with Noah, a smart, loving senior dog with interminable patience ("the best dog in the world," as we put it), I wasn't sure what to expect if a wild puppy—with sharp baby teeth—should move into O's domain. We'd heard that a female would be a good choice for him.

We'd never had one, but why not?

Despite insistent questions that swarmed like agitated bees, I sensed clarity was near, and there was the bark I'd expected. Orion had flushed out another frightened rabbit hiding under our deck. Faster than nearly any zealous dog, a small, gray-tan cottontail sprinted to our back fence, slipped out, and was gone.

Thirteen

FAMOUS OR NOT

Researching dog and cat stories led me to *Rin Tin Tin,* a nonfiction title from author Susan Orlean. The subtitle, *The Life and the Legend,* plus the intriguing cover quote from Ann Patchett, this book is for "anyone who has ever had a dog or loved a dog," convinced me to plan a visit to our local bookstore.

Brookings Book Co. carried used and out-of-print books, so I was optimistic they would have a copy. For a split-second, I'd considered the abundance of used copies on Amazon, but we loved to drift through real bookstores—window displays, actual book shelves, maybe a cat or two wandering the aisles or perched on a cat ladder.

Like an alluring candy store, a welcoming bookstore looks and smells like every book I've ever read or loved, and walking into one, memories rush to the surface, as a sense of divine mystery and anticipation empower the moment. Nothing beats the feel of real paper bundled into a book with a captivating cover and a place to stash an old-fashioned bookmark.

Digital downloads, audio CDs seldom do it for me, so instead of clicking on keys and links, perpetually staring at a screen, I wanted to make a trip downtown to look for Orlean's 2011 book. An inspired option, right? Five, ten minutes, tops, to get there. Even if I had to circle the block a time or two, parking was a cinch. Small town realities have their place.

As a fun aside, and even though I've yet to visit such a bookstore, in my imagination, the best version has a cozy stone fireplace with chairs that look like home circled close for reading, a coffee bar with an impressive variety of tempting pastries, and gently expressive, clearly artistic, violin music weaving a bit of literary magic in the background. Not to be forgotten, the books, yes, the books, are definitely the most important feature. A friendly face behind the counter also adds a certain magic.

The Adventures of Rin-Tin-Tin appeared on television in 1954. I grew up in that era, but don't recall the program. More than likely, however, we (myself and siblings) watched it. I'm also reasonably certain we didn't know that the famous canine was, during a span of star-studded years, not a single regal-looking German Shepherd, but several.

Orlean's bestseller, per online descriptions, is, as you might expect, a "poignant exploration of the enduring bond between humans and animals." The show-worthy Rin Tin Tin isn't the only dog to find fame and fortune, however. Many well-known names come to mind: Lassie, Marley, Benji, Toto, Beethoven, Old Yeller, Uggie, and let's not forget, 101 Dalmatians, Snoopy, Clifford, or Scooby-Doo.

Clearly, there is something wonderfully endearing about dogs.

Each with a story to tell (if they could), canines rely on us to communicate the endless ways they impact our lives. I didn't know, for instance, until reading about "Rinty," that he had been saved from the trenches of WWI. Found on a French battlefield by Lee Duncan, an American soldier, the shepherd's career took off in 1929 when he landed a spot in *Where the North Begins*. Maybe it was those expressive eyes that helped the four-legged actor, beloved by many, snag roles in twenty-seven movies. Not bad at all.

The funny thing is how challenging it is to accurately tell the story of another's life, be it a human life, a cat or dog, or perhaps, a horse or bird. Special moments are forgotten; pictures are misplaced or destroyed; memories are never complete or remotely perfect. In writing this book about our dogs and cats, loved, but not the slightest bit famous like Rin Tin Tin, I tried, above all else, to be a "mindful writer."

Yet, this ever-shifting, rather lofty, destination is mirage-like; the trail is rocky, littered with trial and error, sneaky tribulations, and rampant misgivings. Carlos Fuentes, Mexican essayist and novelist, believed that: "Writing is a struggle against silence." After spotting his quote in *The Mindful Writer: Noble Truths of the Writing Life* by Dinty W. Moore, I mulled it around for some time, because it also explained, in straightforward, eloquent terms, my motivation to write.

Silence surrounds plenty of lives—destroying some, or minimally, inhibiting (or preventing) meaningful communication and relationship equity. Opting for a life of silence may seem like a simplified reality; but sharing thoughts and experiences via books and articles provides insights into the more intricate dimensions of existence, including, as within this book, the revealing human-animal connection. When we fail to seek new information and knowledge on a recurrent basis, we're stumbling about in a heavy fog of "I already know plenty." Curiosity may dim, interests may shrink, and most of all, an ability to learn and grow dies.

As I navigated the perplexing process of getting to the "next dog," I wasn't expecting our process to inspire a book, however. Yet, certain decisions touch us deeply, and then, silence isn't a suitable response. Not for me, anyway. Inclined to put words on paper since penning letters to family members when away at summer camp in Steamboat Springs, Colorado, my younger self—as a sixth grader—already yearned to convey certain ideas in writing.

THE PERRY-MANSFIELD summer camp, established in 1913 by Charlotte Perry and Portia Mansfield, was owned and operated by my alma mater, Stephens College in Columbia, Missouri, in those days. Perry and Mansfield donated the camp in 1963 to Stephens because of their strong performing arts program. Initially five acres, by 1949 the camp had grown to an impressive eighty-eight acres.

Initially focused on the performing arts—modern dance, classical ballet, theatre, choreography, and so on—in 1934, they added equestrian sports. I remember our trail rides, jumping lessons, and a sweet horse that tolerated my so-so riding ability. My medium-sized brown horse was named Annie Oakley or Orphan Annie; I'd have to dig through scrap books in the far reaches of our garage to find out, so I hope you'll forgive my guesswork here.

Swimming lessons also happened—especially leery, at that age, of deep water and diving boards, to my mother's dismay, my youthful interest in swimming was nil—during weekly trips into Steamboat Springs. I recall a modest, old-fashioned main street lined with historic brick buildings—a candy shop, in particular, comes to mind. Ballet was impossible for me with my flat feet; I wasn't drawn to modern dance moves, either. But naturally gravitated to creative cabin projects.

We kept a journal and staged short plays. For *Alice in Wonderland,* which we performed for parents at the close of camp, I was the narrator—an unglamorous role that suited my quiet, but determined, personality. In hindsight, I see lifelong interests taking shape; even though I never pursued the performing arts, per se, I loved writing letters to mail home and watching a story become a play. Every book I've written or read, some kind of story. And poems, all mini- or micro-stories.

Stephens owned the camp until 1991, when the Friends of Perry-Mansfield took over. Still going strong, the performing arts camp of old has evolved into four dance studios, two theaters, two art studios, two writing studios, a costume shop, and a music lab; programs in dance, theater, and equestrian science attract participants from elementary age to college. Additionally, their website now mentions creative writing, and the Colorado Encyclopedia notes an intriguing program launched in 1997—the New Works Festival—to help playwrights jump-start their productions.

Writing this chapter, I had to wonder if there were camp pets, as in cats or dogs, running around. Horses, yes, so I'm guessing there were also barn cats, and friendly watch dogs. Maybe even a German Shepherd or two, like Rin Tin Tin.

Fourteen

A SMALL PHOTOGRAPH

With time to spare before we had to make a final decision, I was leisurely dreaming about puppy names again. An unpretentious black-and-white photograph, barely 3 × 2 inches, of Hannah McCormick, my great-grandmother, sits on my desk for inspiration. In an old-fashioned, ankle-length cotton dress, white with sleeves slightly beyond her elbows, she's holding an open book in her lap. Seated outside, in a simple wooden chair (nothing like the outdoor furniture we see on today's decks and patios), it was summer. Towering, leafy trees behind her led to an open field.

Hannah gazed somewhat seriously, with a squint, at someone wielding a camera. White hair, pulled back, reveals an aging, but still formidable, face; her expression suggests hard-earned wisdom. With a robust build, clearly, she was a sturdy woman of the Dakota prairie, and knew well what hard, repetitive work entailed. Sadly, she'd raised eight children almost single-handedly after her husband died in his early 40s.

Family lore has it that John died from a severe case of the flu. Anna, my grandmother, born in 1889, spoke frequently of her father's death with a sense of longing, but didn't share, or remember, the details.

I'll never know if Hannah (1864–1934) had pets or loved them the way we do, yet, her open, kind gaze leads me to believe it's a strong possibility. Having never met her, though, an air of mystery—a sketchy emotional current—clings to her picture: her modest life of seventy years. Also intriguing, I haven't seen many pictures from the days of old with someone holding an open book.

Was she a reader? Was it the Bible, perhaps?

For whatever reason, Hannah's picture draws me in—continues to intrigue me—and I'd love to unravel her life story. Her December 23rd birthday is interesting, as Anna, her third child as mentioned above, was born December 24, and so was I. Three Capricorns, three generations.

Beyond that, where (and why) was the picture taken? By whom? What was she like? Would I have known her the second our eyes locked? How had she survived the death of her young husband when life, in those days in South Dakota, was mostly about daily survival on remote prairie lands, homesteading, and simple pursuits?

Yet, Hannah's story, like many others, was lost to time. Those who knew her are no longer living; written accounts are scarce. My mother, at eighty-eight, died in 2017, precisely where history dropped me off to figure out the rest of my story on my own. The only thing left behind, a distant path that, inevitably, was forged, and partially defined, by a tangled past that Hannah (Johanna Hannah per some family records) and Anna, her daughter—*my grandmother*—and Patricia, her daughter—*my mother*—experienced firsthand.

Essentially, I suspect, because of the complexities and realities of family lineage, Hannah's story continues with each breath—every piece of my past that I draw on, knowingly or otherwise. Funny how we try to individualize ourselves so heavily, so decidedly, when it's actually impossible. As a temporary manifestation of those who preceded us, as we lean into the next moment and the next, the insistent cycle of life simply presses onward.

"Yes," she said, "I'll have puppies mid-July, for take-home early September." With certainty about availability, I drew a painful blank. Probing, she asked, "Thinking about a male or a female?"

Grateful for an easy question, I said, "Leaning toward a female. We already have a black-and-silver male."

Glancing at Orion, dozing on the window seat, I wondered about Lola. I hadn't seen her around since early morning, but she and Orion weren't exactly "close," so she was probably tucked away in one of her secret spots.

"I can put you on my call list. And when the puppies are here, I'll be in touch."

Relieved a small window of time between "yes or no" still existed, I thanked her, said good-bye. My intuition wasn't tossing up a red flag, and the early summer day pointed to new life, and adventure. As I've mentioned, I'd been down the arduous path of grief after my son's death in June of 2007; my memoir would release in late December, 2015.

The bulk of the work had been done.

An extensive, multi-year journey, I'd learned, during endless rounds of writing, revising, and editing, more about grief than I dreamt possible. I'd also learned about getting to the next morning, through the next day, when all energy and motivation were gone. Such knowledge in hand, I felt more prepared, yet less prepared, for the days ahead, and wondered if Noah's bright, comforting memory could coexist with a happy-go-lucky, wild-eyed puppy—the long-term commitment we'd need to make.

Matthew, by the summer of 2015, had been gone for eight years, and though we never "get over death," we usually find ourselves able to open to life again, one tiny step at a time. So I'd had time to test these turbulent waters, knew that grief, in its myriad forms, *can* coexist with the other aspects of life. Not easily or comfortably for many months, and likely years, but one day, I finally felt able to trust life once more. Willing to bolster a shaky sense of courage and risk the harsh realities of loss in exchange for personal growth, new challenges, and revisiting my capacity for a depth of experience, I'd turned a meaningful corner.

Yet, Noah's death was recent. Our unique bond developed steadily over thirteen-plus years; his gentle companionship had filled a devastating, nearly unspeakable, void after Matthew's suicide. And now Noah, too, was gone. Losses intertwined by history, and something we call time.

Yet, right before my last call to inquire about a puppy, I'd detected a fresh sense of awareness, and was starting to intuit that Noah's sweet memory, instead of only leading to sadness or wishful thinking, had a higher purpose—a much happier purpose, perhaps. By indirectly helping me build a new and caring relationship with our next dog, Noah's spark, like Hannah and her descendants, would live on. So why not tap into the seamless continuum of life, build on the past, instead of focusing on "right timing," well-defined endings and beginnings, when no such thing exists?

I'd believed all along that my heart, my intuition, would lead me in an inspired direction, but I still felt surprised by the clarity of my insight. In nascent form, my ideas had been there all along, but in fuzzy, barely perceptible, ways; and then, they were mired in Noah's absence, not in how he might go on with us in new, heartfelt ways. I realized I was starting to say *yes* to the next dog—cautiously so, with slight waves of hesitation still cluttering the landscape.

But how, I wondered, would (or should) I feel when the moment arrived to say yes (or no) with conviction? Might it be whispered? A quiet nod of acquiescence? Or ideally, would I experience a deeply certain, joyful moment, as important sentiments merged into a puzzle's final resolution?

Walking over to the window, I set my phone aside to spend some quality time with Orion. Slow steps are okay. Sometimes it's the "rush to know" that sets us back. Besides, Orion was here *now,* and as we'd learn one day, much sooner than expected, that wouldn't always be the case.

Fifteen

FINDING HER

Kenyon, a private liberal arts college in Gambier, Ohio, is my husband's alma mater, so we receive quarterly alumni bulletins featuring well-developed articles drawing on the expertise of students, graduates, and professors. One issue easily got my attention: "The Animals in Our Lives: Meet Some of Gambier's Most Cherished Residents."

I admired the small white dog on the cover—dark gray ears, fluffy tail fanning up over her back—sporting a stylish red harness. An eight-year-old shih tzu-poodle mix, Skittles belonged to the college president, Sean Decatur. Skittles had a companion named Roo, same kind of dog, only black, and we see them standing side by side as Decatur leans down to pet them. "Kenyon is a great dog community," he said.

Impressive. And why shouldn't a college campus be a welcoming place for dogs, cats, or other pets? Spending time with them is a source of emotional support, and college can create plenty of stress. Music professor, Dane Heuchemer, pictured with Chloe, a golden retriever, and hound mix, Bentley, aptly notes that ". . . the dog will not ask them (students) if they are ready to take the exam."

Precisely. Animals and unconditional affection somehow soften steep challenges, helping us along more than we fully notice or appreciate.

Other pictures in the Kenyon College publication: Associate Professor of English and three-year-old pug, Heppy (named for Audrey Hepburn); Tibetan terriers, Tallulah and Gracie; Bou and Willow (hound mix), belonging to chemistry professors. I also noticed a turtle, horse, peacock, cow, and a green-eyed cat that looked like a Maine Coon we had (Murry) many years ago.

When Kenyon's costume shop manager found a litter of stray kittens under her deck, she took one to work. Tallulah has been a resident of Kenyon's Bolton Theatre ever since.

Also interesting, a perceptive article about English professor, Jim Carson: "At the Species Boundary." An expert on eighteenth century British literature and English Romanticism, Carson explored the intriguing role of animals in literature while drawing on Human-Animal Studies (HAS), a new and evolving interdisciplinary field that explores the complex relationships between humans and other animals. Carson, shown with his husky, Fergus, shared in the article that, as a kid, "dogs inhabited my imagination."

I doubt he's alone in that regard.

Aren't we all kids again when spending time with our pets? Don't we feel the intoxicating energy and enthusiasm of childhood once more?

Literature and animals seem like a logical and inspired pairing.

I learned that English poet, William Wordsworth (1770–1850), wrote about his dogs, so looking for such a poem, I found "Tribute to the Memory of the Same Dog," wherein he wrote: "Extreme old age had wasted thee away / And left thee but a glimmering of the day."

Wordsworth's mother died when he was seven, and at thirteen, he was orphaned; his adult life was also far from picture-perfect. In 1812, two of his young children, six-year-old Thomas and three-year-old Catherine, also died.

But as he once wrote: "With an eye made quiet by the power of harmony, and the deep power of joy, we see into the life of things." Maybe that's why Wordsworth's work—his esteemed role in the history of literature—endures.

THIS DAY, THOUGH, I WAS ON MY WAY to a small town south of us to meet a five-week-old puppy, the only female in the July litter. The breeder lived on a farm, so we decided to meet halfway between my home and hers; she was bringing a couple of the male puppies, too. Since I was still "just looking," I'd decided to drive down by myself for an initial meeting. Caution kept coming to mind, along with self-talk advice like: *You want to feel certain, excited. Eager to invest time, energy in a new dog, one to love unconditionally . . . for the duration . . . through sickness and health.*

Mid-August, it was a bright, but muggy, day in South Dakota.

John understood I needed to see the puppy without other opinions coming my way. I didn't want to be swayed either way until I'd had a full-blown, unmitigated chance to say *no*.

She's adorable, but, regrettably, I must pass for now. Please keep me updated on future opportunities, though.

We all know the emotional dangers of seeing a bouncy, cuddly puppy, right? But I also wondered if memories of Noah would cloud my vision, or conversely, lead the way? Noticing some anxiety creeping into my thoughts, I gazed out the window at open fields in various states of brown and pale green that hugged both sides of the interstate. A deeper calm, a "no pressure" perspective could only help. I would look. Stay open. Trust myself. *Hopefully.*

My cell buzzed. Waiting until I pulled off at my exit, I figured the text was from John, or my daughter, Erin, inquiring about the highly anticipated puppy meeting. But it was only an appointment reminder.

Turning south at the stop sign, I noticed that the sky was a welcoming summer blue. Scattered, aimless puffs of white roamed freely. Funny how we check out the view overhead as though a gauge of our inner world and the moment at hand.

Storm coming? Anything curious, threatening? A soothing balm, perhaps?

At my destination in minutes, I spotted her vehicle, turned into the parking lot. Pulling up beside an SUV, I glanced over, smiled and waved at the youngish woman in the driver's seat. Despite my anticipation, I planned to stay alert to anything that might point to extra caution. Horrifying, inhumane puppy mills are a sad reality. With no reason to suspect this, I still had to rule it out.

Emerging from our vehicles, we smiled, introduced ourselves and shook hands.

I liked her right away.

"Good to meet you," I said.

"Ready to see the puppies?" she asked. And opening the front passenger door, we peeked in at wee-puppies in a box—three of them snuggled up, snoozing.

"Car ride, they're asleep!" she said, smiling. "They'll come to life instantly when I reach for one."

"I'm sure," I said, quietly. Admiring them, I reminded myself that *all* puppies are cute. And adorable. And lovable. And, *mostly,* irresistible.

"Here's our sweet little female, the only one."

As a nurse who also happened to love schnauzers, held her up, a white fur ball of maybe three pounds with wide-open brown eyes, floppy ears, a touch of a beard, and a docked tail, looked back at me.

"Her eyes, so expressive already!"

I couldn't believe how much they reminded me of Noah's. That same deep calm that seemed to originate from a faraway place that I knew, as well. A place, mostly indefinable, yet known. Instantly, my doubting heart pounced.

"Beautiful, aren't they?" she said. "Such a deep brown."

Reaching out, I stroked her soft coat, and casually, she looked me over, sniffed my hand.

Would she like me? Would "we" work?

Relationship-building was the precise point of it all. Without that, we would both miss out on so much: affection, loyalty, friendship, fun, trust, understanding, the joy and comfort of steady companionship.

"Care if I grab a picture to show John?" I asked, reaching for my cell.

"Not at all."

When a retiring gaze lacking any kind of agenda—innocence embodied—peered back at me with a touch of inviting playfulness, I couldn't help but feel a connection to this puppy. Her photo, perfect. The wild eyebrows, the black nose, that easy look of "don't I know you from somewhere?"

A car pulled in, one left. Parked in front of a veterinarian's office, I barely noticed anything, as I gazed at the cloud-white puppy. Time had stopped.

Should I say yes now, before someone else picks her from the litter, or take a day or two to sort through swirling thoughts with a clear head? How would it feel to fly with the moment, jump in without a second's hesitation?

Lost in thought—heart and head locked in private battle—I finally glanced up, smiled, heard myself utter a few simple, yet, *mostly* unexpected, words.

"You know what, I think she's the one."

Unsure how my ruminating, my hesitation, had formulated a decision, one had surfaced, nonetheless. Somewhere a bell had chimed, and though faint, I'd heard it. Like an answer from a distant and mysterious plane that my subconscious revealed exactly when needed—*not until*—it was a solemn, yet lighthearted, moment.

"You can take her home at about eight weeks, in early September."

Her reply was matter-of-fact, but warm.

Relieved there was time to prepare for a puppy's arrival, I mentioned Hannah, my great-grandmother—how we liked her name and might use it for our new family member.

It fit her; I could already tell.

She didn't need a middle name, but I liked Rose. I loved the play of words, the rhythm and music of lines, pairings, passages. Writing poetry, for me, was an ever-enticing invitation to discover the hidden energy behind a word, a sequence of lines, and the subtle touch of poetry in *Hannah Rose* wasn't lost on me.

S‍un Tzu, an ancient writer, philosopher, and Chinese military strategist, bears a name of honor meaning "Master

Sun." His given name was Sun Wu, 544–496 BC, and he is believed to have authored *The Art of War*. Based on Taoism, his book is, to this day, widely read and studied by many components of society: business, public administration, politicians, management, and military personnel around the globe. His ideas are relevant here: "The quality of decision is like the well-timed swoop of a falcon which enables it to strike and destroy its victim."

Historical accounts of Sun Tzu's life are somewhat "iffy" given how long ago he lived, and the puppy decision wasn't a war maneuver, *or was it?*

Inner conflict, waged privately, is still a "war."

Difficult decisions resemble a hard-fought battle, one undertaken to defeat fear, doubt, uncertainty, and to permit something new or different to arise. The status quo, a formidable foe, pins us to the ground in a flat second. An element of surprise is common to many battles, and this, too, is intrinsic to the decision-making process.

We don't know before we know; we can't be sure until we're sure. Last minute, under pressure, an answer, *the answer*, is often revealed. It's not unusual for the best decisions to arrive like a precious gift from a deeper part of ourselves.

Mysterious, humbling, and unpredictable, there are zero guarantees. When we inhibit the process, things can go awry. Our job is to let go, ride with the unnerving energy of uncertainty for as long as it takes—avoid interfering. *Trust, listen, act.*

AUTHOR LAURA HILLENBRAND, *Seabiscuit: An American Legend,* was also featured in the Kenyon College alumni bulletin. The article, by Julie Barton, author of *Dog Medicine: How My Dog Saved Me from Myself* shared, in interview format, how Hillenbrand had coped with chronic fatigue syndrome for thirty years. Julie Barton, similarly, had struggled with chronic depression, her own health issue.

Coming from a shared perspective, both believed in the incredible healing power of animals. When asked how she connected with animals, Hillenbrand aptly replied, "... they can breathe life into us when nothing else will." For a related question, she added, "Animals address the inarticulate parts of our soul that lie very deep." Her insight, a "capacity to give to us solace," resonated deeply with me, calling to mind my heartfelt appreciation for our four-legged family members.

Something unites us, willingly or otherwise, with animals; studying us closely, they "get us." Perceiving what words fail to convey, gradually, our words also begin to take on value—they listen, learn, try to understand, and respond. But our real intentions are assuredly revealed by tone of voice, behavior, and history together.

Are we, in other words, consistent, trustworthy, caring?

When the Kenyon article was published, Hillenbrand was thinking of adopting a horse named All Around Brown, son of Kentucky Derby winner Big Brown. She met him after a trip to Santa Anita to visit Seabiscuit's old stall. Then a home to Brown, the horse was surprisingly and insistently affectionate with Hillenbrand, a stranger to him, and she sensed "this communion with him." Unseen forces abound. Perhaps, she mused, "Seabiscuit was channeling himself into this horse."

We didn't receive this particular issue of the college alumni bulletin until 2017, but as I read "Authors on Animals: A Conversation Between Julie Barton '95 and Laura Hillenbrand '89," I couldn't help but think of Noah—our remarkable bond from day one—and, later, the puppy named Hannah.

I loved her magnetic brown eyes. *No worries.* My heartstrings—my wavering, somewhat off-again, on-again decision-making process—hadn't let me down, and despite bouts of fear, worry, and vacillation, I'd found my way to the next dog. The war, for now, had been won, and surely, Orion and Hannah would get along. With Lola as their pesky sidekick, life had fallen into place again.

Elizabeth Weinstein's Editor's Page for the inspiring, animal-themed Kenyon College bulletin I've been referencing, includes a picture of Weinstein and Punky, her white dog. She noted that after a troubling diagnosis from her vet, Punky, her beloved bichon frise-cockapoo, had received treatment and recovered. Weinstein, by way of introduction, also mentioned Julie Barton's book, *Dog Medicine,* and how Barton had wrestled with clinical depression in the company of a golden retriever puppy that "rescued her from the depths of despair."

Of course, I thought. We need and respond to such munificent energy—their persistent desire to spend time with us. And caring for them, because it isn't optional, another gift in disguise. Their basic needs can't help but motivate us by inspiring us to keep moving—at a minimum, to keep breathing.

Sensing a kinship with these women, along with others featured in the publication, their rousing perspectives confirmed my impressions about the animals we come to love. Good to know kindred spirits exist. Maybe, after all, the world is a warm, hospitable place; maybe most of us value, love, and enjoy spending time with our humble four-legged friends. A grandiose mental leap? Positive thinking, justified or otherwise, can help; and like that glorious summer day when I said yes to a third dog, a curious and trusting puppy to follow in the mighty footsteps of Noah and Orion, a sizable leap of faith was needed.

As I HEADED BACK NORTH after seeing the puppies, I realized I hadn't checked my cell phone for a reply from John. He trusted my judgment, though, so I wasn't really worried; and besides, he'd picked out Orion without me being there, and things had worked out fine. Knowing someone for a long time has a string of benefits. For one thing, a deeper understanding is born, refined, and nurtured, so when faced with decisions, like a puppy—or something more challenging—tension, complexity, and misunderstandings rarely surface.

The generous speed limit on South Dakota interstates requires drivers to pay attention. My mind was elsewhere, though. Barely going 65 on an 80-mph highway, Hannah's sweet eyes came into focus, as cars and trucks zipped by me.

That hint of shyness, that "I'm all yours" look, was comforting and endearing. I knew John and Orion would love her. Lola, wisely, would tune out the drama, and quickly teach Hannah to "be nice" or keep her distance. I'd seen her set limits with Noah and Orion; she was a firm, but fair, feline.

I remembered wondering how I would feel when I finally came to a decision, but mostly, I felt relief. Getting over the bridge had been rough, but seeing her was the catalyst. Hannah looked like the puppy, the dog, I'd been imagining somewhere in my mind and dreams. Uncanny, don't you think?

Finding our way through thorny periods of indecision isn't a carefree endeavor. Clues are hidden, disguised; fear and anxiety arise to confuse us; we question our intentions, doubt our intuition, and try extremely hard to avoid making a regrettable decision. Then a breakthrough occurs, and we wonder why there had been such a struggle to figure it all out. Like sunlight breaking through heavy clouds, an answer emerges. A furtive, frustrating process that tests our patience and commitment—our mettle.

Traffic was thinning out as I neared my exit. Tapping my blinker, I pulled off the highway and up the ramp to another stop sign before turning west. Passing a field of ripening corn, in the distance, I spotted sky-high cottonwoods swaying in a slight, August breeze. Summer in Dakota. Trees I grew up with along the Missouri River.

At the next stop sign, turning north and thinking again of Hannah, I was excited to see cell phone pictures promised as updates. One other little question drifted free as I pulled into town. Would she, after a few weeks, remember me?

Sixteen

SHE IS A SHE

Have I mentioned I love stumbling across wonderful books and articles that touch my heart, seize it? *The Soul of All Living Creatures: What Animals Can Teach Us About Being Human,* by veterinarian, animal behaviorist Vint Virga, is just such a book (Broadway Books, 2013). Reading his author note, I knew I would encounter valuable insights and keen observations in the pages to come.

Addressing something I'd often thought about, he points out that, though still common in our culture, he doesn't resort to using "it" when referring to animals. Rather, he prefers "he" and "she," as I, and many others, do. Aptly, Virga explains how "it" in this context encourages us to view animals as "objects" instead of "fellow beings." A distinction, he notes, that promotes "them" v. "us" rationalizations.

An expert on the care and well-being of animals, to him "all living creatures . . . are unique and individual beings."

Isn't this obvious? Can you imagine thinking of your dog or cat or horse—a living, breathing animal—as an *it?*

If in doubt, Virga's book explores his premise through captivating stories that reveal the profound connections between humans and animals. It's distressing to consider the statistics around the "care" of animals. Vast numbers euthanized on a routine basis (approximately 1.5 million each year according to ASPCA, American Society for the Prevention of Cruelty to Animals); overwhelmed shelters struggling to offer viable alternatives to ending innocent lives. As the ASPCA website points out: "We Are Their Voice." Virga reports in his book that some 70 million animals live as strays—200 million worldwide according to the World Health Organization—and possibly more troubling: "another 30 million die every year of neglect, cruelty, and mishandling."

Discouraging, and undeniably tragic, I often wish we—one couple with modest resources—could do a great deal more. As Mark Twain told us: "If you pick up a starving dog and make him prosperous he will not bite you. This is the principal difference between a dog and man." Was he right?

Poet Mary Oliver, in her wonderful collection, *Dog Songs* (Penguin Press, 2013), also reminds us of the special bond between humans and dogs. After sharing her life with beloved canines, Oliver manages to transform familiar moments into insightful mediations on how we interact with them and what they teach us.

"A dog can never tell you what she knows from the smells of the world, but you know, watching her, that you know almost nothing." Erudite. Staying open to the humble role of perpetual student, we have so much to gain. Edith Wharton captures a heartwarming truth with this: "My little old dog—a heart-beat at my feet."

When we view dogs through such an accurate lens, it's virtually impossible to deny them status and caring and love—to discount them as "just dogs."

John Muir also illuminates this compelling landscape: "Any glimpse into the life of an animal quickens our own and makes it so much the larger and better in every way." Born in Scotland in 1838, he was a naturalist, writer, and advocate for United States forest conservation. Also the founder of the Sierra Club, Muir played a major role in the development of Yosemite and Sequoia National Parks.

Migrating to America at eleven years of age with his family, Muir authored *Stickeen: The Story of a Dog*. Based on his second trip to Alaska in 1880, he explored Brady Glacier (now Glacier Bay National Park) with a friend's dog. Considered a "great storyteller," Muir initially put down his adventures with Stickeen as a short story; in 1909, though, he published it as a book—one that became a "classic dog story."

Apparently, Stickeen, described as a small black dog (pictures I've seen, though, show a tan, black, and brown collie-size dog, a Scotch shepherd mix, perhaps), which Muir wasn't that keen on initially, revealed himself, during their hazardous journey, as a worthy and welcome "dog-friend."

Muir also noted that ". . . through him as through a window I have ever since been looking with deeper sympathy into all fellow mortals."

On Goodreads, John Muir's timeless story earns high praise: a well-loved tale; an exhilarating story grown into an American classic. Reportedly, Muir found *Stickeen* difficult to write, but feeling so strongly about his message, persevered. The Sierra Club website notes that during his grueling journey with Stickeen, the author came to believe that our "horizontal brothers" are not that much unlike us. Brothers, indeed, and dog-friends. Anything but "pets." (In this book, as you know, I use the familiar term only for purposes of simplicity, not because I believe it accurately describes the animals we bring into our homes as family members.)

On a related note, recently, on a program reviewing the accelerating growth of companies selling pet-related products, they were talking about the "humanization" of pets. It's definitely big business, and far from the right emphasis. Caring about animals isn't about making them more "like us"; rather, it's about recognizing and respecting their natural needs—their innate way of being—and not trying to turn them into human clones to suit our silly notions. Even a 2008 article in *The Seattle Times* (Lifestyle), in turning to dog expert Cesar Millan, suggested that this steady trend (noted previously as anthropomorphism) can be overdone.

Millan, commonly known as the dog whisperer, recommends: exercise first (they *are* dogs, after all, and can't be expected to live sedentary lives), setting limits using "calm, assertive leadership," and affection. He worries that some pet owners tend to favor affection, almost exclusively, when learning how to behave is also important. *Balance* is key, isn't it? An overly aggressive (and inappropriate) emphasis on rules and altering normal dog behavior can become horribly abusive; complete disregard for exercise can become blatantly neglectful; forgetting, or failing, to care is a form of cruelty.

When I see a dog dressed up in child-like clothes, this, for me, is a blatant and troubling form of humanization. Even cat attire is available. Do an online search; it's all out there. Designer options, apparel for pets, and so on. Our dogs may wear a holiday collar for a Christmas card, and when frigid winter weather dips to twenty below with heavy snow and wind, we probably put a warm coat on them.

Otherwise, I just don't get it. Dogs and cats aren't dolls, and they sure aren't children. *They are animals.* We can love them, care for them with heart and soul, without twisting reality. I know we can.

IN HIS USUAL EAGER, JOVIAL STYLE, Orion greeted me at the door when I returned home from meeting the lovable, puppy-version of Hannah. He never grew tired of this happy routine: the ritual of running to the door, barking excitedly, and wagging his tail. Sometimes Lola joined in, while also trying to stay clear of Orion's antics, his high energy.

Carefully maneuvering her way toward me with her big motor going and circling around my legs, she loved to have her say, too. Neither Orion nor Lola—neither he or she—constituted an "it," of that I was certain. I reserve "it" for inanimate objects like lamps and chairs and buildings, and avoid "it" for perceptive, wise-in-their-own-way animals, that are admirably content with life's basics, and a chance to brighten our days.

"Hi, Orion," I said, looking down so our eyes could meet. Leaning closer, I stroked his coat, waited for his excitement to subside, and seeing Lola determinedly coming up from behind, I made sure to acknowledge her, as well.

"Loved the picture," John called from the kitchen. "Sticking with Hannah for a name? Did it fit her?"

"Better than imagined," I said. "Wait till you meet her in September, she'll fit right in. I still can't believe I said yes. I hadn't planned to dive right in, you know."

"Sometimes we just know," he said, tossing a kitchen towel over his shoulder.

Disentangling myself from Orion and Lola, dropping keys and purse on a small table near the door, I walked out to the kitchen. I hadn't been gone long, but it felt like a day or two. We talked about Hannah, then decided to take a walk with Orion. The neighborhood was reasonably quiet, and spending time outside felt like pushing the reset button. A puppy would be joining us soon; new group dynamics would take time to reveal themselves. Maybe we wanted to cling to the moment—to the past—for a few more days. A walk would give our emotions room to breathe, let the soothing green of summer inspire us.

Martin Tupper, English writer and poet in the 1800s, made a memorable point with this: "Well-timed silence hath more eloquence than speech." I knew our walk wouldn't be of the silent variety, not totally, anyway; but time outside with Orion, with nature in the forefront, reliably opened a comforting emotional space—a time cushion, so to speak, where problems faded, perspective deepened.

THE NEXT MORNING, though, I woke up in a slight panic. Some might call it buyer's remorse; others might call it the customary aftershock following a difficult decision. But, painfully, and yet again, I wondered—still in an early morning brain fog—if I'd romanticized the idea of a puppy, conveniently minimized the demands of caring for a young dog once again. Bringing her home only three months after losing Noah was, without question, chancy. Not the extended pause I'd originally felt necessary.

How did we get here? Will it work out? What if it doesn't? Had I made a serious mistake deciding on her so quickly? Would Orion accept her? How would we find time for new-dog training, vet visits, and what about keeping up with her activity level and need for supervision?

Sleep was no longer possible.

I got up, grabbed a robe and headed for the kitchen. Surely coffee would help. I'd been over these random fears multiple times. Knew them by heart. Knew none were worthy of more time or energy. Yet, habitual, lifelong reactions, like fear and worry, die hard, if ever.

Lola found me in the kitchen, moseyed over to say good morning. She must have had plenty of food, as she wasn't in her customary rush to have me fill her dish.

"Hi, girl," I said, with a lingering sigh, but just reaching down to pet her helped me curtail my silly, wildly spinning thoughts. Fresh coffee, its powerful aroma, also helped to remind me of other mornings when our simple and comforting routine was in the forefront. When Noah and Orion, exuding no worries, had dozed, heads touching, on our window seat as though friends for life.

Pouring a cup, adding a splash of cream, sitting down at the kitchen table with the morning light peeking through our eastern windows, I quietly, but firmly, told myself: *it's a puppy,* not triplets, a dangerous African safari, open-heart surgery, a wedding or a funeral. Perspective is really all we have to lean on in moments like this, and fortunately, wise words from Alfred Lord Tennyson came to mind:

"Sometimes the heart sees what's invisible to the eye."

I *knew* bringing Hannah home was a path filled with heart; at a bare minimum, she needed a family to love her, care for her. I also *knew* that logic and reason can only propel us halfway down the street; then, without fail, we are forced to rely on something considerably more ethereal: higher instincts, gut feelings, a whispering, yet insistent, intuition. My heart had seen what was invisible to the eye; my heart had seen Hannah.

Lola on my lap, purring loudly, was the perfect antidote for last-minute jitters. Sipping my coffee, I regained a sense of calm. It was okay to feel excited about the puppy with the warm, trusting eyes. Like Noah and Orion, Sidney and Lola, she would be the next star member of our no worries club. *I knew it.*

I'd once read that when unmonitored, the mind is like a wild river, and mine had fallen prey to this dynamic as night had turned into morning. Fortunately, in letting go of my unease, a comforting childhood memory surfaced: delicious blueberry pancakes with blueberry syrup that my mother had made for us as kids. We loved, in particular, the silver dollar cakes. Lined up on a hot griddle, us watching for bubbles to form so she could flip them, we were worry-free, I'm sure. Not a bad way to live at any age.

Picking up Lola, I went to look for some blueberries in the pantry. Tucked in our cookbooks are many of the cards my mother sent us—thank-you notes, thinking-of-you notes that shared new or updated recipes. Special memories, remnants of yesterday, can ease our fears, distract weary minds—even rescue us from ourselves.

Seventeen

CARROT CAKE

The blueberry pancakes, as things turned out, were merely the start of a baking binge that seemed to arise in the aftermath of my Hannah-Rose-is-coming-soon jitters. Creative solitude with fairly quick results is often the star of my emotional health wisdom when it comes to "getting a grip," "finding center," or "staying calm in the face of change." Meditation, reading, writing, and time with nature are part of my arsenal. At the core, it comes down to remembering that life is always about the basics, nothing more, nothing less. On a spiritual level, *this is Zen*.

Does anything unsettle us—or simultaneously, excite us—as much as change? Showing up on our doorsteps in thousands of slick guises, it arrives with or without warning, with or without our permission or bidding. Luckily, kitchens—the precise, sometimes challenging, steps cooking and baking require—offer a pleasant psychic space for reflection. A convivial place to drift with feelings, ideas, or intuitive waves of awareness, both John and I gravitated to open, sunny kitchens.

So when an overcast Saturday arrived, leaving it slightly cooler for late August, and we'd already been to the farmer's market—came home with tomatoes, cucumbers, okra, fresh herbs, carrots, eggs, and a couple of homemade cookies—John took Orion for a long morning walk, while I watered young trees, shrubs. In the front yard, a lemon-yellow potentilla that bloomed nonstop from early summer to fall; in the back, mostly trees, and our towering white and pale pink hydrangea.

Only hardy varieties survive South Dakota heat, wind, and erratic rain showers during the heart of a sweet prairie summer, so keeping up with rapid weed growth was an ongoing issue—they survived no matter what. Luckily, the weeds couldn't compete with our prairie grass. Planted in our front garden and along our north fence line, it reached skyward in graceful, almost billowy, waves, thriving under our intense, no-nonsense summer skies.

Priorities out of the way, I'd decided to focus on a three-layer carrot cake using gluten-free flour. We'd made, and loved, Bobby Flay's recipe, and I'd had good luck with gluten-free flour in other cake recipes. So we were optimistic about this little experiment. Flay's recipe used three forms of ginger—crystallized, dry, and fresh—a pound of grated carrots, crushed pineapple, and toasted pecans.

On top of that hefty concoction, and between layers, when baked and cooled, there is a marshmallow fluff cream cheese frosting. When done, calories and all, the cake looked like it came from a bakery. At least, carrot cake includes some "healthy ingredients." Before starting my baking project, we put together a late breakfast—the very traditional bacon and eggs—and then I gently ushered John from the kitchen.

"The cake will be done *when?*" he asked, before heading to the garage to start the dreaded lawn mower. "Can I get the yard mowed first?"

Sometimes we bribed ourselves in small ways to push through our least favorite yard and house projects. (If you want to give it a try, it usually works!)

"With cooling time, it may be late afternoon before we can sample it," I replied. "But you picked a good day to mow with the overcast skies, and I'm sure O will be out to help you." Orion loved to tag along while John mowed. Watching, waiting, he wanted to be included in whatever was going on.

"A long time to wait," he said, asking me to toss him a bottle of water from the refrigerator. "But somehow, we'll make it."

We laughed, and I uncovered our yellow stand mixer. Slipping the paddle beater in place, I retrieved three, eight-inch baking pans from the cupboard, and as tedious as it was, prepared them exactly as instructed before setting the oven at 350.

Before, when making this recipe, I'd taken some shortcuts on pan prep, but that had backfired in a seriously regrettable way. The recipe suggested two, eight-inch rounds, but I opted for three to get thinner layers; that minor change in the recipe worked out fine, as long as I adjusted the baking time.

As I sifted two cups of gluten-free flour with the other dry ingredients, Lola strolled into the kitchen, looked up at me, purring, as usual.

"Hi, sweet Lola, where have you been this morning?"

Finding the blue rug in front of the refrigerator, she made herself comfortable. Our animals, dogs and cats alike, loved to join us in the kitchen, and unless we were in a big hurry in our small, square kitchen space, we enjoyed their company just as much. Noah and Orion loved vegetables—everything from kale and spinach to carrots, peas, and green beans—and apples and banana pieces were also popular. Popcorn, minus the salt or butter, was another treat our dogs loved.

Orion liked to jump and snag a piece midair.

Cracking three eggs into a small bowl, I heard him bark. Perched on the window seat, he'd probably spotted John pushing the mower across the front lawn.

Next, I added a half cup of almond oil and two teaspoons of vanilla to my mixing bowl. As the ingredients started to come together, I remembered a quote from Roald Dahl's book, *Charlie and the Chocolate Factory*. Something about being "a great deal luckier than we realize" and "usually getting what we want—or near enough."

We'd been lucky to find Hannah, so why worry in the face of good fortune, love is love. Besides, what could be better than an amiable puppy face—for us, for Orion?

Sinking into a comfortable, everything-will-be-okay feeling, I finished the cake, poured a reasonably even amount of batter into buttered and flour-dusted pans—in the bottom of each, parchment paper also had been buttered, dusted—and slipped them in the oven.

Orion, patiently waiting by the door, was next. Running outside to "help" John mow the back yard, he was a bright and happy picture of health, vitality. His shiny dark coat was quite a contrast to the sweeping green of summer. When John saw Orion racing toward him, he stopped the mower, reached down to let him know he was appreciated, loved. I never tired of watching them interact.

The primal pleasure of connection, the honoring of life energy, the celebration of friendship, all on full display.

I loved to linger with the seemingly small, happy details of life—fleeting expressions of joy that are timeless and real and possess a hidden power to transcend the routine nature of existence. With Noah and Lola and Orion, we'd enjoyed an abundance of such moments, but it's important to catch them when they occur by looking into the deep well of mortality—with a steady, unflinching gaze—to witness and fully appreciate life energy, *life forms,* at play.

Pulling myself from the glass, I noticed Lola still dozing on the blue rug.

After I fed her, freshened her water, I noticed the carrot cake was starting to smell sweet, indulgent, and curiously comforting. Like encountering a collection of special memories, I was reminded of birthday cakes, wedding cakes, and holiday cakes. Occasions marked by sugar, flour, butter. Not the healthiest fare, but in moderation, quite enjoyable.

Pouring a glass of tea, adding plenty of ice, I pondered my next step.

Frosting a cake while still too warm was a common mistake, so I decided not to make the frosting until the cake was out of the oven, the layers safely cooling on racks.

LABOR DAY 2015, a day that felt more like mid-summer, rolled around. John, busy with our yard, wanted to make sure it was "puppy ready." They consume everything in sight, that much we knew. John didn't enjoy yard work, either, but over the years, we'd managed to spend plenty of time doing just that.

After taking a serious interest in the semi-neglected yard that came with our house, our overly ambitious efforts generated, as a bonus, an unending need for trimming, weeding, watering, and fertilizing.

During high school and college summers, John worked for a golf course in Ohio that his grandfather had purchased as a retirement project. And like our yard, the course needed mowing, watering, and trimming on a continual basis. Way too much of a good thing, I'm guessing. Although, on the bright side, he has cherished memories of working on the golf course with his Uncle Buzz and Aunt Dee.

As John puts it: "I couldn't goof off much, learned a lot."

Waving, I pulled away from our driveway.

"Can't wait to see her," he called out, in gloved hands, holding a rake. Glancing toward our front window, I saw Orion taking it all in. Looking and listening, while quietly reminding us that words aren't always necessary. Pausing to look or listen, we are more deeply aware, fully present. Animals, though, have a stark advantage on us. I haven't met or known an abundance of humans who know when or how to stay quiet for long. Talking, our default setting.

Turning at the corner of a tree-lined residential street called Victory, I glanced over at the passenger seat—the cardboard box with a blanket and soft, cuddly toy. Would she sleep during the ride home, or want to camp out in my lap? Mere days shy of eight weeks, I hoped she would sleep. I'd thought about bringing a crate or small carrier, but decided against it last minute.

In new surroundings, I doubted she would be all that lively.

Hannah, a heartening leap of faith, was a new dog for a new day. As a fun extra, she might resemble Noah someday. Reassuring thoughts paraded through my mind, as I considered my checklist one last time. But the highway, like the sunshine and stunning blue sky—lulled me. I was ready for this exciting chapter to begin. And I knew we would love her no matter how she looked—like Noah, or not at all. Since meeting a very young Hannah, I'd studied her new pictures several times. The cute factor, of course—plus the chance to be sure once more—but her snowy white coat, intelligent brown eyes, and gentle gaze made us smile with each text.

Turning right at my exit, heading east, I remembered the Bobby Flay carrot cake from a few weeks ago. Gluten-free flour worked well; we couldn't even tell the difference. A good omen, we'd decided. Change, taking risks (even minor ones), and exploring intriguing elements of newness honor the mystery of existence, so why not engage with life in positive, uplifting ways?

Carrot cake in mind, I took a long, calming breath, tapped my blinker and turned into the parking lot. After pulling to a stop near the right car, I glanced over at the woman behind the wheel; smiling, we waved to each other like old friends. I felt like an impressionable young girl on Christmas morning. Anticipation and wondering, gifts and bright colors, holiday trees and flashing lights. All of this and much more wrapped up in this moment, on this gentle, early September day.

Emerging from my car, I noticed how blissful, how freeing, it felt to overcome unfounded fears, cumbersome doubts. Recognizing that feeling from past experience didn't make it any less meaningful now. Finding and maintaining the stamina to move forward in any context is a unique, demanding journey. Gravity and history and fear forever trying to pin us down.

The next few minutes went by in a blur. We talked about food, shots, grooming, and so on, while Hannah watched and listened. Before long, I was holding her, and after we sorted through a few more details, I opened the car door, put

Hannah in the small box with comforting words of welcome. She already knew her name, which smoothed the transition. Her eyes held wells of trust, curiosity, new energy yet to be claimed, explored, and celebrated. Like discovering a lock's secret combination, I felt our connection click into place.

The days ahead would be filled with trial and error, learning, and love. Hannah would get to know us, and her shyness would melt like spring snow drifts. Food and water, squeaker toys, puppy chews, and a cozy bed would help. Safe haven, in other words. Building strong relationships, with animals or humans, can't be rushed or overly engineered, but a natural process respecting the gradual nature of learning and generating trust usually works.

Starting my car, I backed out, drove less than a mile west to the north exit. She hardly moved. Didn't sit up in the box, or attempt to find a way out and over to my lap. Looking at me with an open, comfortable expression, like we were old friends, when I talked to her, she tipped her head—curious, but not concerned or anxious. Hannah, in fact, seemed calm, cool, and collected.

Taking her lead, I brushed aside any flicker of fear about Orion and Lola, how they might react to our newcomer. In days prior, I'd wondered if Lola, at fourteen, would resent the relentless pace of a puppy, or if Orion, our high-energy guy with a tendency to assert his agenda, would be eager to convey his seniority and status.

Glancing over at Hannah again, silently, in her language, I tried to reassure her that she was going home—a place where she would be loved, well cared for, kept safe. If I was anxious, she'd surely pick up on that, so I reached over, stroked her head, and then looked for some music on the radio. Classical, New Age.

We had a couple of CDs with soothing music specifically for pets. During road trips, time alone at home, or during nasty thunderstorms, they helped. Wishing I'd brought one along, I landed on a classical station, instead, just as a long stream of impatient cars passed me. Labor Day traffic. At least fewer semi-trucks were out.

When we pulled into town, Hannah's eyes were closed. Like the steady motion of the car, music worked. Caving in to sleep despite her efforts to stay awake to study me and her new surroundings, she couldn't have looked more relaxed.

MERE WEEKS AFTER NOAH DIED, I'd read W.S. Merwin's Pulitzer Prize-winning poetry book, *The Shadow of Sirius* (Copper Canyon Press, 2009). Named poet laureate by the Library of Congress on two occasions, Merwin's budding talents surfaced when only a boy. Though his father, a Presbyterian minister, wasn't someone the famous poet admired or even pretended to "like," he wrote simple church hymns for him at the tender age of five.

Merwin dedicated part two of *Shadow* to his beloved dogs: Muku, Makana, Koa. Born in 1927 in New York City, in 1977, he set his sights on Hawaii. Purchasing an abandoned pineapple plantation—eighteen acres near Haiku on the north shore of Maui—he tirelessly transformed and healed the mistreated ground by planting and caring for thousands of palm trees.

The Merwin Conservancy, a nonprofit organization Paula and W.S. Merwin founded to preserve their home and palm forest, reported that the restored land features some 3,000 palm trees with more than 400 taxonomic species, 125 unique genera, and nearly 900 different horticultural varieties. Not your average backyard garden, the Merwin palm tree forest is one of the "largest and most extensive palm collections known to exist on earth." An incredible accomplishment that's difficult to fathom in terms of sheer dimension and positive environmental impact, Merwin, a humble and retiring poet, also left us a viable blueprint for the future.

His last poem in part two of *The Shadow of Sirius,* "Dream of Koa Returning," is vivid, endearing, and accessible. He writes of "long amber fur" and "listening to the river." Like sitting there by him, as I read his poem, Merwin's affection for his dog Koa was tucked within each line—beautifully, and poetically, of course. Another of his poems, "Variation on a Theme" (*Collected Poems,* 1996–2011, Library of America) ends with "and the dogs who are guiding me." Clearly, the acclaimed author, who (as I later learned) died in March of 2019 at 91, shared my deep conviction that our "pets" are so much more than "pets."

A good relationship with them stirs something primal within us—something we feel we've known forever. I've long believed that if we try to separate ourselves from this powerful reality, we cut ourselves off from the very life force that animates all living creatures. Then, what's left? Inner estrangement comes to mind. A denial of what's obvious, natural, and real has consequences and lasting impact.

Like Merwin's incredible palm tree forest, he understood that ignoring the earth, our living planet, will cost us dearly as the years unravel. *Reality is reality.* Try as we might, we can't outrun it or dream it away.

HITTING A FEW STOP SIGNS into town, Hannah began to stir. Eyes open, she looked at me as though waking from a wonderful dream. I hoped we would deserve her trust, loyalty, and affection: things we would have to consistently earn one day at a time. No shortcuts, no assumptions, no excuses.

Turning north on Park Avenue (yes, I'm afraid we're still in South Dakota, not New York City) and driving north toward Victory, I remembered another timeless voice. Poet Walt Whitman wrote: "This is what you shall do; Love the earth and sun and the animals, despise riches, give alms . . . ."

If we love the right things, how can we ever really lose?

Eighteen

HANNAH'S WINDOW

So how do we come to see the world anyway? One might say we have an inner window: a captivating, intricate mosaic of everything experienced, imagined, seen, or discovered. George Bernard Shaw, Irish novelist and playwright, had this to say: "Better keep yourself clean and bright. You're the window through which you must see the world."

I thought about this idea as I studied Hannah perched on our window seat like she'd lived with us forever.

Wondering how a curious puppy of ten weeks views the busy and complex world beyond the glass, "Hannah's window" came to mind. Not *just* her window, of course: Lola, Orion, Noah—all of them loved a chance to gaze beyond the glass. Just like us, most animals get restless and bored when forced to stare at four walls all day. But Hannah, it seemed, immediately gravitated to that sunny, padded ledge, especially when our house was quiet.

Invariably, I would find her there—dozing with her toys, or watching anything that moved on the outside. Sometimes she peered out at an ordinary scene—trees, houses, snow or sky—contentedly observing whatever was there.

Optimistically, or naively, or both, we also assumed that Hannah was our *last puppy*, so why not call that special place—our sunny eastern window—Hannah's window?

When we moved on to a different home, or sat in cozy chairs by a warm, evening fire in our advanced years happily reminiscing about the dogs and cats that were good enough to share time and love with us, we could easily pinpoint history with those two words.

So what does a puppy "think about" when hanging out on a cozy window seat to peer beyond the glass? A world unknown, yet known, perhaps. We can never know their thoughts (do they ponder funny humans, food, weather, long walks, imagine a carefree life in the wild?) or dreams (research indicates they dream about "us," their family), yet, we can infer quite a bit by watching them. A little mystery is okay, too.

I MONITOR A COUPLE OF schnauzer rescue organizations via social media. Sometimes there is good news, sometimes not. Lots of senior dogs, or dogs that owners can no longer care for, looking for homes. Dogs with eyes that reveal the whole story: sad, defeated, weary, frightened, anxious, lonely. Seeing the pictures, reading the posts, "home needed" or "needs help" or "rescue available," I want to reach out with a kind word, at least. Innocent creatures ignored, abandoned, neglected, abused. Yet, more puppies are born each day, more schnauzer puppies, as well—some will find loving, caring homes, many will not. How can we change this troubling reality?

I wish I had an answer; I wish human nature wasn't so insensitive and fickle. Wishing doesn't help much, though, and such traits, plus all of their nasty cousins, are everywhere on this spinning planet.

Would it help if no one ever bought a schnauzer, or any other kind of puppy, from reputable breeders? Not a chance. Dog shows are here to stay, so no longer breeding dogs and cats is about as likely as a world that stops investing in thoroughbred race horses. Puppy mills, however, are a serious problem, and if reputable breeders went away, wouldn't they rush in to fill the gap?

A nonprofit organization devoted to global animal rescue, SPCA (Society for the Prevention of Cruelty to Animals), in 2014 estimated the existence of up to 5,000 puppy mills in America—the majority in the Midwest. The Humane Society of the United States believes there are closer to 10,000 puppy mills in operation. Certain states have been identified as more likely to house hidden operations that function on a despicable, uncaring shoestring.

Regulations vary. Enforcement is erratic.

So, understandably, such disturbing money-making schemes persist, while imprisoned animals suffer enormously for an entire existence.

Moral of the story, for now, at least, is to rescue a dog or a cat whenever possible; support organizations dedicated to the humane care and treatment of animals. And don't hide from this devilish issue. Be certain you know *where* your next cat or dog comes from. Do research, interview other people who purchased a puppy, a kitten, from your source. Along these lines, even in your own neighborhood, open your eyes, trust your instincts, stay vigilant and closely observant.

If you never see a dog outside playing or running or enjoying some fresh air, take the time to wonder why; if you hear harsh, hateful screaming directed at a dog, a pet, take action. If an animal cries out in pain, pick up your phone. Take a picture, a video, get a recording. Call your vet; call the Humane Society or animal control; call anyone who will listen. Confide in *someone*. It's really not difficult to imagine what happens behind closed doors, when your observations are troubling enough.

How could living conditions, conveniently concealed by walls, be any better?

Intuition is a great resource. Tap it; trust it.

A friend of mine was once a pet-sitter. She cared about animals, took her job seriously, but inevitably, she encountered situations that were less than ideal. This is reality, unfortunately. As nonprofit organizations committed to humane animal treatment remind us: "We are their voice."

Granted, when we take action, things may not improve drastically. People deny reports of ill-treatment, of course, but *trying* to impact a troubling situation is the very least we can do. Conversely, things may improve greatly for the animal. The owners may realize they aren't up to the task, find a rescue society or a new home where the pet is appreciated and loved. Happy endings exist.

"Taking Hannah for a short walk," I said, snapping on her collar, grabbing a leash.

A warm September morning, it felt like my favorite autumn memories rolled into one moment, one day. Scattered leaves blanketing lawns, sidewalks, driveways. Artistic shades of red, orange, yellow—some vibrant, some faded, curled.

John was working in his office. Orion was probably asleep near his feet in a new dog bed he'd claimed as his the second it hit the floor.

"You two have fun," he said, coming to the bottom of the stairs. "Orion and I will be up in an hour or so. Lola's down here somewhere, too. Probably sleeping in the bedroom closet on our best blankets."

We laughed. Dogs and cats can find the nicest, softest, cleanest blankets in the house, right? Discerning taste, you could say!

Lola had several new hiding places since Hannah's arrival some two weeks ago. Consistently adept at finding a soft, quiet place to nap, was a cat thing, I guess. One morning I looked for her, on and off for a couple of hours, until I found her in a guest bedroom under a nightstand—a place I'd never seen her before.

Resourceful, I thought, knowing this was her way of navigating a new animal in *her* house: a rambunctious, impervious puppy learning and testing limits.

Still getting a feel for a puppy collar, a leash, and leisurely neighborhood walks, Hannah's button eyes danced with quiet energy as we headed out the door. Playing with leaves, picking up a stick to carry with her, barking at anything that dared to move or make a sound, spelled Hannah on a walk, so far.

Getting to know us, her new home—she loved being outside for any reason.

Orion, at her age, had been a far different story.

Firmly sitting down in the front yard as we tried to get him up and moving, he didn't gravitate to collars, leashes, and quiet walks. Gradually, though, he caught on. Training treats offered along the way clarified things for him, I suppose.

A block down the street, Hannah found a rather long stick. Quickly retrieving it, the stick clenched between sharp baby teeth, we walked on. Reaching for my cell, I called her name for a quick picture. A fluffy white dog of six pounds or so, head held high and looking proud of her bounty—it totally looked like she was smiling. A few feet later, though, I offered a fair trade: a peanut butter puppy treat in exchange for the stick. Worked like a charm. (Even a small twig can cause harm to a dog if you wish to research it.) Hannah, luckily, was okay with our impromptu swap, and our walk resumed. Soon enough, she found another stick—*of course*.

I wondered how or why I'd ever had a single doubt about committing to a puppy. On this blissful autumn day, my fears made no sense; even Orion had welcomed her without incident. Day one, we took them out in the backyard, and John tossed out a toy to see what would happen; surprisingly, they began playing like best friends.

We soon noticed, however, that Hannah, *definitely our last dog*, wasn't remotely shy anymore, and insisted on taking toys away from Orion at every opportunity. A perfect gentleman—*what a surprise*—he gave in, easily. Not the slightest bit combative or aggressive, he stood back, waited for her to dangle a toy near him, then politely engaged in another round of tug-of-war.

As we walked on, Noah's image came to mind several times. Never seeing the ending that lay in wait, I'd walked him on this same sidewalk only months before. Finally, though, I stopped thinking, let the moment, and Hannah, sweep me away. It was enough, more than enough. A simple moment in time when there really was nothing to worry about. I'd have plenty of time for that—tomorrow.

RELICS OF THE PAST. Sometimes they arrive without warning, yet with perfect timing. In this instance, it was a well-worn book from John's childhood. By Al Perkins, the title immediately resonated: *The Digging-est Dog*.

What dog doesn't love to dig? A Beginner Book from Random House, Perkins' book was published in 1967. I'd never heard of it until seeing it at John's home many years ago. Complete with colorful, sometimes comical, illustrations by Eric Gurney, the book jacket was faded, taped and torn in places, and quite literally, falling apart. Powerful signs a book—one his mother mailed to us, along with other childhood treasures—had been loved.

So I sat down to read it.

Hannah was asleep in her crate; Orion was in the backyard catching some late afternoon sun. On days like this he loved to stretch out and snooze on an old blue rug on our deck. Lola, also asleep, was on the couch, curled up in the sunniest spot she could find. *Smart animals.*

I opened to the first page: "I was the saddest dog you could ever see," the author began. On the floor, beneath a bird cage, and chained to a hook on the wall, sat a sad-looking brown dog with black ears and patches of white, and a "for sale" sign hung on the wall.

What child wouldn't be captivated from the start?

Duke, a city dog, was living in a pet shop while waiting for a home, and finally, when Sammy ventured by, he got one. Taking him to their family farm, the "country dogs" discovered that "city dog Duke" didn't know how to dig. But he learned, and quickly. So much so that things went seriously awry when he dug up the entire farm, then a nearby town. After a series of humorous escapades, at last, a cheerful ending arrives.

What is it about a good children's story that touches something in readers of any age? Closing the book, I remembered *Go, Dog. Go!* by P.D. Eastman. Published in 1961, many believed the book was authored by the widely celebrated Dr. Seuss. No matter such details, my children loved the fun, high-action text and illustrations. Teaching color, relationships ("Do you like my hat?"), and ideas via busy, lovable dogs had a joyful appeal. Besides, what child isn't intrigued by something called a "dog party"?

The narrative, set to music and performed on a stage for the Seattle Children's Theatre, evolved into a popular play performed for children all across the country. Also part of the Beginner Books series launched in 1957, *Go, Dog. Go!* followed many familiar titles. A book by Dr. Seuss, pen name of Theodor Geissel, got things rolling.

The Cat in the Hat sold a million copies in its first three years alone. Kids went for Seuss (1904–1991) like bowls of sugared cereal. Receiving a Pulitzer Prize for a Lifetime of Contribution to Children's Literature in 1984, the cartoonist, writer, and poet seemed to rely on humor, animals, and a keen understanding of human nature to communicate our complicated world to young readers.

The manner in which he gently nudged their imaginations was pure genius. And the longevity, for instance, of *How the Grinch Stole Christmas!* is nothing short of remarkable. A holiday classic surfacing frequently in yet another movie version, is loved by the young and impressionable, the cynical and discerning, the old and infirm. What is your favorite scene? Are you a fan of redemption in such stories?

LOLA STIRRED ON THE COUCH, stretched and yawned—that deeply peaceful yawn only cats can muster. Was she overshadowed by our dogs? I wasn't sure, but we hoped we gave her the same amount of quality time, attention. A napper deluxe, if I was resting in the afternoon—joining the likes of Thomas Edison, Lady Gaga, Einstein, John F. Kennedy, Salvador Dali, and my *wisest* friends—she, invariably, found me, and purring, like life was perfect in every way, snuggled up next to me.

At night, same story.

Finding me reading in bed, she'd curl up near my head and purr relentlessly until she felt the urge to move on. Food, water, a trip downstairs to her litter box—maybe a little privacy in one of her hideaways. She'd been my close companion since the long-ago day when I spotted her hanging from my window screen that warm autumn afternoon in St. Louis, and Megan, many weeks later, had carried her to our door asking: "Can you still take Lola?"

I HAD PLENTY OF WRITING to do (books rarely write themselves); fall yardwork was never-ending; numerous household chores—laundry, dishes, cooking, trips to the grocery, cleaning—also came to mind, as I added the tattered children's story about Duke to a sizeable stack of books in our living room.

I also made a mental note to track down a paperback, adapted and illustrated in 1997 by Iza Trapani, of a beloved story from my childhood memories: the "doggie in the window" tale. Patti Page's recording of the song, released in 1953, was a hit song my mother introduced me to as a child. I remembered its lively melody and catchy lyrics about a "waggely tail" (yes, that's how they spelled it!) and hoping that "doggie's for sale."

John and I loved to share things, like books, from our past. The years before we knew each other felt like another lifetime. One set apart from our relationship, yet, a transformative chapter that established personalities, early beliefs, interests, and fundamental values. In many respects, childhood conditioning.

Worlds with similarities and differences, plus all things down the middle; worlds slowly woven together in innumerable ways. Ups and downs, misunderstandings and confusion, clarity and joy. Moments that imperceptibly deepen in significance; memories diligently carved in the vanishing sands of time.

UNCANNY, BUT WHEN THINKING about John, he seems to call or show up early from local appointments or business trips. This afternoon, no exception. Still adding up all the things I should be doing, I heard the rattle of our garage door. He'd run out for a haircut and birdseed for our feeders.

"Hi," he said, "back early."

"I see that," I said, as we shared a hug, a kiss.

"Here's the mail, pretty exciting stuff, as usual." We laughed at the junk mail we received and instantly recycled. "Only one envelope worth opening."

Orion was at the slider, barking his greeting, wiggling with excitement. Hannah, clearly ready to get out of her crate, chimed in.

She loved playing with Orion. Wrestling was their "thing," and tugging on a toy to determine the lucky victor. Squeaker toys, part of our lives since Noah's arrival, were always in demand. After a tip from my daughter, we saved squeakers from worn-out toys to stick in our pockets, keep by the back door, or tuck inside an old sock and tie a knot for a "new toy." Convenient for calling in our dogs from outside, we also used squeakers to let them know it was time to stop barking, or to help calm them during storms. A familiar, trusted noise worked wonders.

JOHN OPENED THE DOOR for Orion as I flipped through our mail. Nothing worthwhile except a larger envelope that actually held some interest for us. Setting it aside for later, Hannah's insistent whine and puppy bark were letting me know it was time to get her outside. In the throes of house-training, time was our dependable enemy when we failed to pay attention.

As soon as I opened Hannah's crate, Orion hurried over to sniff noses with her. Watching them—Orion in his curly black coat, Hannah in long, unkempt white—I thought, *We don't have a multitude of busy dogs like they did in* Go, Dog. Go! *and our dogs don't wear hats or drive cars, but we can have a dog party. A simple one with Kongs filled with frozen yogurt, diced carrots, and tiny dog treats.*

Taking Hannah outside, I laughed at my daydream. Realistically, though, I knew that Doggie Day Camp and Doggie Day Care programs were popular all over the country, and were probably places that held carefully orchestrated dog parties. Hard to imagine, but if dogs liked them, why not?

LATER, TOWARD EVENING, as the sun slid from a western sky, I found Hannah curled up on the window seat again. John and Orion were out walking. Lola was asleep in my office on a blanket under my desk, and our smart puppy already knew exactly where to go when things got quiet.

A three-inch fluffy yellow duck with a squeaker, of course, lay near a front paw. Smiling—there was that cuteness factor again—I recalled that unopened piece of mail; its contents would reveal Hannah's "family tree," her lineage, so to speak. Even dogs and cats have a past, right? Ancestors, generations prior, that led the way. Most unidentified, but there, nonetheless.

Considering the past, those who walked before us, I remembered some piercing words from my favorite poet, Alfred Lord Tennyson: "The quiet sense of something lost." Why is it that when change happens, when our personal landscape shifts and sways around us, an undeniable feeling of loss also springs to life?

Whatever is new, in a good, bad, or mixed way, also points with equal fervor like a laser to that which is missing: things, people, places that have been lost. Noah, no longer here—his rightful place on the window seat newly occupied—came to mind. Wishing I hadn't noticed that "quiet sense of something lost," I knew it was intrinsic to the sway and swagger of time, to how we cope with endings, beginnings, and the steady flow of all things painful and joyful, abundant and scarce.

The ultimate life pairing, I suppose it's a compulsory kind of harmony—one we'd rather shun. Yet, remembering Noah, how he'd held us up after Matt's loss—heavy-feeling years that lingered in the aftermath—reminded me of the countless events and moments when his comfort, his quiet presence, were nothing short of lifesaving. Reminiscing also made this moment *complete*. Not sad or happy, black or white, but more importantly, complete and true.

Deeply, profoundly, true, like Noah's peaceful gaze and rumpled beard—his warm and generous nature, innate intelligence, and tireless affection.

Time had come along, upset the status quo and challenged us to weld the pieces back together. A fluid process without destination, really, but one thing was clear: Now, it was Hannah's window. I would get used to seeing her and Orion there, just as I'd gotten used to seeing Noah and Orion there. And sometimes Lola. Maybe, one day, we really would have a dog party in Noah's memory.

I'd make a cake for dogs—box mixes sold online looked easy—and buy pointed party hats. Such hats and festive scarves that say "let's pawty," along with squeaky toys from Zippy Paws that resemble a piece of cake with a candle in it, are also sold online or in various pet stores. Not to ruin the party planning idea, but I struggled to imagine any dog or person getting much out of such "human hoopla."

Franz Kafka looked at it like this: "All knowledge, the totality of all questions and all answers is contained in the dog." If true, I was certain John and I, party or no party, were in outstanding company.

Hannah stirred, as if reading my thoughts.

Satisfied to see me standing there watching her, she closed her eyes, turned back to sleep. I loved—and envied—her easy contentment. The question, and the answer. Hannah couldn't have known it, but for us, she was definitely both.

In case, like me, you're intrigued by the Kafka quote, it's from a short story he wrote in 1922. "Investigations of a Dog," published posthumously in 1931, was later released in London in 1933 following the first English translation. The story, told from the perspective of a dog, an unnamed narrator, considers the "nature and limits of knowledge." Apparently, Kafka delves into philosophical questions while exploring the dog's mind, but there are many interpretations of this story—some, in fact, are fairly interesting. Several minutes of research, and you'll get the idea.

A collection of his stories, *Investigations of a Dog: And Other Creatures,* is available in paperback.

GLANCING OUTSIDE, I SPOTTED John and Orion heading up the walk. Synchronization came to mind. Stepping together like longtime friends, the harmony—the unity—was apparent. Would Hannah sense them, or sleep on?

Watching Orion in his cherry red harness, I couldn't foresee all the trouble ahead, but for some reason, I tried my hardest to freeze the moment in time.

We miss a multitude of such moments, don't we? *Busy, tired, stressed, forever distracted by past and future.*

This time, though, I soaked it all in: a warm autumn dusk, a man I'd loved for many years walking his spirited dog—layers of curled and worn leaves underfoot—a cloudless sky, the perfect canvas for star-gazing, a puppy named Hannah asleep on the window seat, and a well-loved cat in the next room.

I would check out the stars later on.

Frequently, we looked for Orion—majestic and mysterious against a black night cap. A winter constellation, visible in the Northern Hemisphere September through March, it was time to start checking for it again. The grandest of all constellations, according to some, did you know the middle star in his sword is the Orion Nebula where brand new stars are constantly born?

As they came through the back door, Hannah stirred.

Signs of life were seldom lost on me. Even routine, expected ones: an ear twitch, a tail wag, a gentle, excited growl when playing or greeting us, cat tails swishing back and forth in warning or if sizing up a chirping bird, a down-dog stretch (yoga style) in the morning, a bearded head tipped to the sky to sniff the air after a rainstorm, napping with one ear up, one down, the animated bunny hop when chasing after something, or snorting during a fierce tug-of-war.

Maybe a happy pant after running or playing hard, the bored, indifferent yawn, listening or curious eyes, the well-timed bark. And what about the heavy sigh before sleep? What would you add?

I wondered if this was a long list, or a mere fraction of countless, observable moments that magically occur when cats and dogs are loved and valued and intrinsic to the swirl of motion called life.

ONCE WE FACE SIGNIFICANT LOSS—human, animal, friend, or family—these wondrous signs of life touch us ever more deeply. We *know* what is "here now" will vanish one day with or without warning; we *know* each second is dear and precious and, in the final analysis, all we will ever have—so we can't help but notice such moments with greater appreciation. The exact opposite of trite, they are powerful and real. Never make-believe, but true; never commonplace, but inherently special.

Most of all, these moments aren't incomplete, they're wondrously complete.

Venturing down from the window seat, I watched Hannah navigate the carpeted, three-stair pet ladder. John had made it for them one Christmas, and now, a new puppy was taking her turn. Slowly and deliberately, Hannah made her way. *Signs of life.*

Nineteen

STAR WARS REUNION

Up before the sun, John or Orion, Hannah or Lola, as usual, I glanced outside at the sky. Coffee was next. We'd picked up a twelve-ounce bag of medium roast at the Cottonwood—our coffee shop on Main—so I hoped for something blissfully aromatic to pull me forward into morning.

John and I were far from stuffy, dog snobs insisting on a certain pedigree; rather, we were dedicated free spirits who happened to love dogs and cats, ours included, of course. But as I sat down with my coffee to learn more about Hannah's "family," I wondered what I would find. A quiet, sleeping house made for peaceful reading, so with Lola purring on my lap, I reached for my glasses and finally got around to opening the American Canine Association envelope. Contents, as expected.

An official seal, lower left, gave the certified pedigree document an authentic look. Next, holding a computer-generated map of four prior generations, I quickly scanned the array of names.

Reading at the dining room table, I was soon lost in the creative names, the colors, of the males and females that preceded Hannah. But one word sprang to mind as I studied the diagram: *uncanny*. Smiling, I laughed out loud. We loved her, weren't remotely concerned about lineage except in terms of her health, but such things were still fun to know.

On a whim, we'd done the paperwork for Orion, too. I'd framed the certificate, hung it near our back door next to a canvas of John and Orion hanging out in the backyard on a hot August day. A priceless shot that captured the essence of their endearing connection, I glanced at it nearly every day. In an aqua polo and khaki hat, John was on one knee in the overgrown summer grass holding grilling tongs and chatting with Orion. Smoke billowed up behind him.

Orion, stretched up tall on hind legs, had one paw on John's knee, the other near a shoulder, with his head twisted to one side, probing John's eyes. Pure luck that I got that shot, I loved it—the way it captured a trusting playfulness, how it revealed the mutual affection I witnessed between them every day.

Such a great pair, I *knew* they would be together for many years.

Passing through the back door on my way to my car to run some errands, heading out to water the garden or go for a walk, I also paused now and then to look at Orion's American Kennel Club certificate. It was fun to read the names of his family: Bjorklund's Alexander the Great, Hope Like Kallie, Turtle Creek Bright Penny, Max B Cooper, Kallie Racer, and Madison Baby Racer.

But this morning I couldn't take my eyes off Hannah's certificate.

Uncanny. Totally eerie. Seriously fun.

When we filled out the paperwork that transferred ownership from the breeder to us and requested her pedigree, a limited number of blocks were provided to print her name. With four extra spaces after Hannah Rose, on a whim, we added L E I A for Princess Leia of Star Wars fame. Silly, yes, of course, but now, scanning all the names that preceded Hannah, it seemed otherwise.

Still early, were my eyes deceiving me?

The diagram began with Sir Reggie of Howe and Dolly Jean Howe, but the prior generation included "Buddy Luke Skywalker," a puppy from "Kelly and Tina's Darth Vader" (not kidding!). Skywalker was white; Darth Vader, naturally, given the movie, a black schnauzer. One dog in Hannah's lineage, "Precious Sasha," was salt and pepper like Noah. Somehow, without knowing anything about her heritage, we'd added another Star Wars character to the mix. Mere coincidence?

Breeding names are rarely commonplace; clearly, this was an interesting, and surprising, discovery. Other names on her chart: Frisco's Snowangel, Silver Bullet VIII, Ace N The Hole, Precious Smokey, Little June Bug. So what were the odds of Hannah Rose Leia having Luke Skywalker and Darth Vader in her family tree?

We weren't superstitious, but I knew John would appreciate the unlikelihood of Hannah finding her "Star Wars family" just because we'd added four more letters to her name to complete empty boxes on a form. I took a sip of coffee, glanced down at Lola, now asleep, and wondered if this was mere happenstance. Could curious forces of destiny have put these pieces together for us—this humorous thread connecting past and present?

If nothing else, it was an amusing mystery to ponder as the sun edged its way skyward. The locally roasted coffee—Colombia, notes of "sweet, lime, honey, and toffee"—had lived up to our expectations. Bright, lively, and slightly earthy—one of life's small comforts.

I couldn't wait to tell John, a big Star Wars fan, about Hannah's "family." We'd probably have fun asking ourselves what actress Carrie Fisher, aka Princess Leia, might have ventured about our discovery. Thinking about this, only one thing came to mind: "May the force be with you, Hannah Rose Leia."

Twenty

STARRY NIGHTS

Just like people we've all known, schnauzers are "talkers." When they "see something," they "say something." Part of their breeding, part of the package. So while we work on limiting their innate need to "talk," and/or "bark," we aren't at all interested in succumbing to our country's "no barking" obsession. *It's out there.* Sadly, some can't tolerate any noise or natural canine behavior—their dogs, never allowed to "speak," in other words. But unlike a demanding, conformity-laden culture and society that prefers to ignore the true nature of things, dogs bark to *tell us something.*

We can't imagine not permitting our dogs to be dogs. Beyond ridiculous, this nutty, narcissistic (cruel?) expectation points to something else: as a species, we don't like to listen. Sure, we "talk" endlessly—in person, by text or phone, via blogs, social media outlets, music and songs, newspapers, books, or journals, and so on—without bothering to listen: deeply, with our full attention.

Is it possible that barking dogs, like a mirror image, simply remind us of ourselves—our incessantly busy, preoccupied, inherently noisy culture? Like us clutching our smart phones or habitually listening to MP3 players in headphones or ear buds, most dogs are social and conversant.

So for anyone who can't tolerate barking, yet insists on having a dog, here's an idea for you. Instead of a living, breathing animal, consider buying a lovely dog statue—metal, plastic, wood, granite, clay, bronze, glass, marble—for yard décor. Lots of options online. *Think about it:* low-maintenance, silent, attractive.

I STARTED MULLING ALL of this around, rather sarcastically, I'll admit, during another baking venture. Drawn, this time, to a bittersweet-chocolate tart for Mother's Day, I'd studied lots of tempting recipes, but settled on one coined "outrageously elegant." Sounded like a worthwhile challenge. My crust—almond flour, cocoa and so on—was done, ready for the next step. Pressing it lightly into my tart pan, I trimmed excess dough from the rim and popped it in the freezer so it could firm up before baking.

A blissfully mild day, we had our windows open, and periodically, I'd hear a dog bark—reliably followed by someone yelling like a crazy person in the background. A human bark, if you will. Not surprisingly, I much preferred the dog's bark.

Isn't there something dreadful about a loud, abrasive human voice? A dog is merely communicating her world, what she's noticing, but screaming adults (or kids, youth) are a different story entirely. What are *they* communicating? Stuck in a useless, reactionary pattern, I wondered if they realized how they sounded—like something sharp, grating against a chalkboard.

Do they believe that unleashing a burst of negative energy is *training?* Funny, right?

When frustration, impatience, and impulsive behavior take flight, nothing gets "fixed" or "changed." Sounding firm or direct is one thing, part of living with any dog; but yelling like the world is ending is inappropriate and hopelessly ineffective. Read most any article on the subject. The stark opposite of positive reinforcement, temper tantrums can cause an animal to feel disliked and unwanted, not to mention the confusion and anxiety that befall a creature subjected to the constant irritation of a shrill, harsh voice.

BAKING AND COOKING OFTEN eased my mind from troubling issues like this, but today, windows open, it wasn't working. Hard to tune out dogs and impatient humans, roving lawn-mowers, and such, but I was also worried about Orion. He'd been experiencing brief bouts of abdominal upset: times when he couldn't relax and looked uncomfortable. We'd consulted with our vets, had medication for symptoms, but we still wondered what was going on with him.

Only four and still a young dog, surely, we reasoned, it couldn't be anything too serious. His appetite hadn't changed; he wasn't vomiting or lethargic.

Pulling my crust from the freezer, I lined it with parchment paper before adding a jar of uncooked beans so it wouldn't puff up while baking. Why go out and buy pie weights when dry beans worked so well?

Checking to be sure the oven was ready, I set the timer, slid the tart shell inside.

John had taken Orion and Hannah outside for a game of fetch, and Lola was on the deck in her soft crate with mesh sides. She loved being outside, and this way, we didn't have to turn her loose to get lost, run over, or otherwise injured. She napped, watched the dogs, birds, squirrels, or the occasional rabbit. When she managed to exit a door—a real Houdini—she preferred to relax in a quiet spot under our deck. Cool and dark had its appeal, I guess.

The tart filling came next, but I wasn't in a rush, so I pulled the iced tea from the frig, poured a glass for John, and headed outside for a short break. The weather, intoxicating: greening trees, light breeze, billowy clouds adrift on a raft of blue.

Hannah, then Orion, ran over when they spotted me emerging from the house.

I had some banana chips (crunchy dog treats without added sugar) with me, so after handing John his tea, pulled a few from my pocket.

"How's O?" I asked. "Seem okay, comfortable?"

"Nothing unusual, and he's keeping up with Hannah!"

At ten months, she ran and played endlessly. We marveled at her clever tactics to engage Orion. Patient and accommodating, except when food or napping were on his agenda, they were a surprisingly good fit. When they sat or napped together on the window ledge, they created an artistic image of black and white.

"Maybe," I said, with a noticeable sigh, "we should take him in for tests." I hadn't forgotten Noah's gall bladder issue, and *something* was bothering him.

"He's young, looks great, but infrequent, reoccurring symptoms without a known cause aren't our imagination. Tests, yes, I suppose."

"Looks like they could use a drink." They were panting, and the sun felt strong for May. We had limited shade in our backyard. After removing a row of aging trees that were no longer thriving, we'd planted new evergreens—three Norway Spruce. Handing my banana chips off to John, I went to get water. "Then," I said, glancing over at Lola, "the tart project beckons."

Hannah ran over to us about then—twig tucked in her mouth, as usual—and John handed me his glass. She couldn't have looked more at home.

Tossing her a green Air Kong, she dashed off. Our best fetcher, by far. Noah and Orion, never terribly keen on catch and retrieve, used to look at us like "what's the point anyway," but Hannah loved it. Curiously, she also gravitated to every toy and dog bed our male dogs had shunned, ignored. She also loved the four-foot dog ramp we had built for Noah as part of our deck when he could no longer do stairs well, but Noah had seldom used it. Neither had Orion. Hannah, however, had a penchant for whatever they hadn't liked. Who could explain it?

Back inside, I paused again to watch Orion in a fierce tug-of-war with Hannah over another popular toy: an orange ball with a giant loop on each end. Perfect for pulling and yanking each other around the yard. Good exercise, and O looked fine. Totally fine. High energy, shiny coat, bright eyes. Trying to push away a flurry of fears, I remembered my crust was on a timer. Five minutes remained, luckily, so I ran a bowl of cool water outside, before retreating to the kitchen once more.

Moments later, I sat down with the recipe, but had to read the instructions for the filling twice. The crust, baked and ready to go, was cooling on a rack, but I couldn't focus on the recipe. Cream, milk, bittersweet chocolate, sugar, cocoa powder, eggs—ingredients that must be combined in the proper sequence. A new recipe requires a little more concentration, and I could tell it was going to be a struggle, so I thought about freezing the crust, finishing the tart when I had my heart in it.

Maybe once we knew more about Orion.

Reaching for my glasses, I diligently, and to no avail, poured over the recipe yet again. Details weren't sticking, so Plan B won out: cool the crust, wrap it tightly in plastic wrap, store it in the freezer. For now, calories spared.

JOHN HAD A BOOK CALLED *365 Starry Nights: An Introduction to Astronomy for Every Night of the Year*. Orion was featured in the chapter called "January." The bold hunter faced with a charging bull, had three stunning stars in his belt that were sometimes known as a "belt of pearls." And for some, years ago, the constellation signaled "stormy winter weather," to others it was a promise of "goodness and light." Which would it be, I wondered.

Twenty-one

SHOWGIRL

Lola loved cat nip, so we planted it under a tree or potted it for her. A perennial that takes plenty of sun, she was drawn to it like bees to the hive. Exploring it, she'd sniff it, roll around in it, but she never bothered to nibble on the aromatic leaves. Rubbing her face in it, she reveled in its earthy smell. Cat nip, or catmint, an herb, isn't something every cat finds euphoric.

Nepetalactone, an essential, volatile oil, is what gives them a five- to ten-minute "high." Harmless, nonaddictive, cat nip arrived in America via settlers who packed up their entire lives and carried them across the ocean.

Lola, however, white face, charcoal nose with egg-shaped patches of color under her ears, head and whiskers nestled in it—front paws in pots of leafy green—looked the picture of contentment when "under the influence." Eyes closed, lost in a world of her own, as the sun dipped farther into the western horizon, we'd sit on the deck with a glass of evening wine, a shared Guinness, to watch her.

Lola's health had been remarkably steady and uneventful, with the exception of a recent ear infection that responded well to medication. Our affectionate girl from our St. Louis days seemed timeless—the wise old friend with no intention of leaving anytime soon.

By 2017, she'd outlived Noah by nearly two years, but at sixteen, clearly, Lola had reached her golden years, and my internal clock warned that another ending was surely in the offing. I'd heard of cats that lived to be twenty, but how often, I wondered. Watching her carefully, monitoring food and water intake, I treasured special moments with her. Walking into any sunny room, odds were good I'd spot her stretched out, lounging in those heavenly rays.

But when it comes to cats, why are some people so bothered by these smart, sun-loving creatures? We have some neighbors who rescue cats, give them a good home, sometimes five at a time, but John and I have friends and relatives who disappear when a cat is around. I've never understood it.

Albert Schweitzer, 1952 Nobel Peace Prize recipient for an ethical philosophy known as "reverence for life," wouldn't have understood it either. As he once wrote: "There are two means of refuge from the misery of life—music and cats."

The famous (controversial?) novelist H. P. Lovecraft (1890–1937), in fact, penned an essay about the ostensible superiority of cats. Information about *Cats and Dogs,* possibly no longer in print, is on Goodreads: the reviews, a mixed collection of funny and serious. But this Lovecraft quote, in particular, summed things up rather well: "The cat is such a perfect symbol of beauty and superiority that it seems scarcely possible for any true aesthete and civilized cynic to do other than worship it."

He also adored cats because of their notable sense of contentment. One of their more admirable qualities, Lovecraft explains that cats know how to be "alone and happy," easily finding ways to entertain themselves; he described felines as "cool, sure, impersonal, and delicately poised." Animals that "never slobber."

Cat-lovers, dog-lovers, was he serious about all of this or, mostly, having some fun? One of many authors who preferred the refined company of leisurely felines, Ernest Hemingway, another cat-lover, made this observation: "A cat has absolute emotional honesty: human beings, for one reason or another, may hide their feelings, but a cat does not." Point well taken.

Artist Leonardo da Vinci believed: "The smallest feline is a masterpiece," and Jean Coteau, artist, playwright, poet, said: "I love cats because I enjoy my home; and little by little, they become its visible soul."

AFTER THE SECOND ROUND OF ear medication, I noticed that Lola was losing weight; her appetite seemed "off," given her love of food. Definitely sleeping more, she began to have trouble keeping her food down and was making frequent trips to her litter box. The medication, was it too much for our very senior cat, or were the sands of time merely depleted?

We talked about what to do. Prolong her struggle or give her a peaceful exit, a release from physical ailments and deepening woes. We wanted what was best for Lola, despite our sadness at the thought of losing her. Poignant images of the tiny white kitten clinging to my office window screen rolled through my mind.

Seemingly, she'd always been there—a cheerful constant through the ups and downs of good news, bad news, our moves from St. Louis to Indianapolis to South Dakota, claiming each new space without hesitation or concern. If she could find a sunny window, a dish of her favorite kibble, all was well with sweet Lola.

Who hasn't heard the popular Barry Manilow song, "Copacabana"? Story lyrics—by Jack Feldman and Bruce Sussman—fueled Manilow's composition of the hit song released in 1978. "At the Copa," named for a New York City nightclub that Manilow frequented, is about Lola, a Copacabana showgirl, a boyfriend and bartender, Tony, and gangster, Rico, who makes a play for Lola. All does not end well, however, as Tony dies in an ugly foray with Rico, and a grief-stricken Lola never recovers from her misfortune. Read the lyrics sometime to learn exactly how things went down!

Needless to say, we'd always associated our Lola with the catchy tune. She was our "showgirl," now facing her closing days—her time with us, and everything she'd loved about life as she knew it. Sleeping under the Christmas tree, nuzzling a pot of cat nip, chasing after a rogue mouse—once, when one found its way into our home, Lola made it an urgent priority to seize the pesky intruder—lounging in comforting rays of afternoon sunlight, or dozing on my lap. What had I missed? What might she add to this necessarily human list?

BOTH OF US TOSSING AND TURNING, we'd gone to bed planning to take our girl to the vet in the morning. A Saturday, we'd have to be able to get in before closing time at noon. She seemed almost okay in some respects, and not at all okay, in other ways, and even though I sensed we were facing the end of a cherished relationship, I couldn't help but hope for a brighter morning. We'd set her up in a cozy spot with everything she needed: her soft bed, food, water, litter box. Used to roaming freely at night, we weren't happy about keeping Lola downstairs, but we knew it was the safest option.

Her meow, that night, was strangely soft, almost plaintive, and we'd considered an after-hours emergency vet visit, but given her age and quirky symptoms, decided to wait. So often, animals, like humans, gradually improve; plus, we knew we would opt to keep her comfortable, rejecting involved diagnostic options or hospitalization.

Lola deserved a peaceful transition, if nothing else.

I nudged John.

"Still awake over there?" I asked, in a whisper.

The third week in May, our window was cracked for fresh air and invigorating predawn bird song.

"How long have you been awake?" he asked. "I dozed off for a few minutes, but that's it. Wonder how she's doing?"

"Should I check on her?" I didn't want to disturb her if she was sleeping, but then again, what if she was in pain? That, I wanted to know.

"Didn't really seem like she was in pain."

"I know. But maybe she's stoic, like our dogs."

Silence was all we could come up with, and waiting.

I planned to check on her as soon as I got up, and would call our vet the second the office opened. Getting up at five had its pluses. But we were still restless, and I could almost hear our worries making a troubling racket of their very own. If we were honest with ourselves, precious little reassurance probably existed.

I thought about Orion's strange symptoms last summer.

When we'd taken him in for tests, we'd hoped for a good report—reasons to move on, not worry so much about his periodic abdominal upsets—but instead, we'd heard all about pancreatitis. Tests and symptoms pointed in that direction.

Fairly common with schnauzers, we switched him to a prescription dog food and low-fat treats.

Carrots, apples, blueberries, strips of kale, or small pieces of boiled, unseasoned chicken, were okay, but smaller, more frequent meals (four per day) also were part of his new diet. High fat, in other words, or eating too much at once could trigger another painful attack. We'd witnessed two such attacks—repetitive vomiting that wouldn't stop—that required emergency trips to the vet. An injection that stopped his vomiting, along with fluids for dehydration, worked quickly, but some animals need hospitalization when their pancreatic attacks can't be brought under control.

So far, we'd avoided that.

With the exception of a few minor upsets, Orion had responded well to his new food, and things were looking up. Still such a young dog, we were extremely relieved when it wasn't a fatal diagnosis. Yet, we had to be very careful, and setbacks could occur for various reasons; but optimistically, he was playing with Hannah, walking every day, sleeping well, and giving us no real cause for greater concern.

Lola, I feared, wouldn't be so fortunate. A spirited showgirl—a gentle friend and beloved family member—very little reverses the insistent aging process.

Rolling to one side, I glanced at the clock on my nightstand. Nearly midnight. Our room was quiet except for O's light snoring. Sleeping by John's feet, sometimes, like most dogs, he made funny noises while dreaming.

Do they really dream about "us," or are they mostly chasing down other animals, hunting prey? Hannah still slept in her crate—a place she'd grown fond of with its memory foam mattress (good for joints), snugly blankets, and soft toys.

O also loved his super large crate (why cram dogs into tiny, cramped and undersized crates? A safe place, *their home*, why not provide ample space for them to move around when confined?), but when Noah died, he decided it was time to take his place. Uncanny how he'd never complained about sleeping in his crate until we buried his friend, then he sensed an opening. And a new place to sleep.

Experts don't recommend this practice, of course.

I remember working on an allergy question involving Noah. A veterinarian with a specialty in dermatology asked us what kind of material was in his bed. Any wool blankets, for instance? "Could you describe what he sleeps on?" she asked. Smiling to myself, I'd admitted, that his bedding was "a lot like ours." We didn't have a wool bedspread, though, and Noah curled up on an old cotton blanket, so we laughed and quickly ruled out any potential problems with wool.

MORNING FINALLY DAWNED, AND I took a deep breath before walking downstairs to check on Lola. The second she heard me, a quiet meow, then another. Relieved, I flipped on a light, and immediately spotted her, curled up in her round bed.

"Lola," I whispered, "doing okay?" Of course she couldn't respond, and of course she wasn't "okay," but a fuzzy morning brain lacks details and awareness.

Another meow, with a faraway ring to it. Definitely not her usual greeting.

"Lola," I said again, hurrying over to her, "let's go see if we can get you some help."

Morning brain: unsure, rambling, useless.

But I knew she loved hearing my voice; it comforted her and that was something. I reached down, picked her up, and held my old friend close—her worn, weary body shaped by her years, the generous amount of time we'd spent together.

Still purring, Lola dozed, seemingly resigned to whatever happened next.

My intuition pushed me toward the inevitable; I listened, but resisted. Different food, a miracle drug—maybe something within reach that was reasonable, hopeful. Yet, part of me knew we were saying good-bye. A deeply private moment, a sacred passage, had arrived.

Our journey, our relationship, a close and comforting connection, had somehow led to this very day. Granted, cold hard facts hadn't been stared down; painful final decisions hadn't been articulated. Still, we *know* before we know, don't we?

Existence, a timeless space hovering wildly, where the past and the future blur together as one, has only to wait for us to step into the truth of it all.

Twenty-two

SLEEPY EYE AND LINUS

I once posted a question on Facebook that struck a nerve. Comments were prolific, reflection and longing apparent. Social media at its best, really. When people who aren't lifelong friends, but often acquainted solely through a social channel, can converse about something meaningful, deeply relevant, and insightful. This was my question: *Was your childhood filled with books and laughter?*

Comments were quite varied, some were lengthy and forthcoming. A surprising number wrote, "no books, no laughter," or something along those lines. Another set wrote "yes" to books, but "no" to laughter (or vice versa), but only about a third remembered enjoying both. Emotional undertones surfaced frequently: a sense of sadness, regret, even bitterness. Lucky ones, in my estimation, conveyed appreciation and joy, sharing that they had grown up with plenty of books, trips to the library, and an abundance of laughter. Books and laughter, essential to a lively, warm, and supportive childhood environment.

A noticeable wistfulness radiated from some comments—those who felt cheated along the way. Many of them, to compensate, had made a point of focusing on books and laughter as adults, parents, or grandparents. Some mentioned angry parents and a painful absence of laughter, an absence of books, and how they'd wished for both as children.

Funny how the basics resonate so strongly with us in terms of quality of life.

I grew up with books, to a point, but definitely sought them out on my own once I'd experienced our Carnegie library, and we enjoyed some laughter. More is always better, though. Many parents or caregivers seem to err on the side of being overly serious and/or demanding. Yet, so much of what happens in any given day is funny, if we possess the wisdom to acknowledge and celebrate it.

Books and laughter, magical ingredients at any age—childhood, adulthood, old age—aren't high-dollar items, either. There's something about levity, a jovial, kind, loving perspective, that lightens the mood, gives us energy, and imparts a sense of well-being. And books. How they exquisitely nurture the mind and spirit, especially during our formative years when we are happily curious, and life is shiny and new.

Huddled in the children's section of an old stone building in the center of town, as a girl growing up on the prairies of South Dakota, I poured over stacks of tempting books I couldn't wait to check out and read. Library card in my pocket, I knew exactly how many I could take home. But which ones would I choose? Such a delicious question for a young mind. Stories about animals, dogs, cats, or horses, often won out.

Who, for instance, didn't love *Black Beauty*, the 1877 novel by Anna Sewell?

Sadly, she died mere months after its publication, but, at least, she knew her famous book had taken flight. Disabled and unable to walk for most of her life, horses became her dear friends—a primary impetus for writing her only novel. Sewell, a literary pioneer who broke from traditional literary form to tell a story through the eyes of a horse, has never stopped inspiring readers.

Advocating for horses in Victorian England—pushing for humane treatment, better care—Sewell continues to teach generation after generation about the unmitigated value of living creatures. As anti-cruelty efforts took off around the globe, her impact spread far and wide; we simply never know where our ideas and accomplishments will lead.

THE SUMMER AFTER WE lost Lola, buried her near her old buddy Noah and the rock garden we'd planted in his memory, Hannah, now three, jumped in the car, and we headed east to New Ulm, Minnesota.

Like Noah, she loved road trips. If she could smoothly maneuver her way to my lap, that was her perch of choice; but Hannah also liked to plant herself between us—hind legs on the edge of the rear seat, forefeet on the padded center console—to "smile" and take in all the sights. A smart girl, she liked motion and a window view.

We've seen car seats or safety belts for pets, including a new model promoted on *Shark Tank* not long ago. Undoubtedly a safe and sensible option for many pets, we planned to study our options, ask around, before purchasing something. Restraining an animal comfortably can't be the easiest thing in the world, but if you use them, like them, bravo. A safe pet is always best.

"Do you think we'll like the house?" John ventured, as we crossed the border into western Minnesota. "Looks great in the pictures."

"Bigger than we want, and then there's Minnesota and its taxes." We laughed. South Dakota didn't have an income tax, while our progressive neighbor to the east had rather steep tax rates. "A change is appealing, though. Ten years in a cul-de-sac has obvious drawbacks. Some nice people, but increasingly claustrophobic."

Laughing, we talked over the house we were planning to walk through, its exceptionally generous lot with plentiful trees, perennials, and open space. No yard fence for Hannah, but we could quickly remedy that. All things considered, it sounded promising.

Glancing around to the back seat, I saw her dozing on a blanket, chin resting on a stuffed toy—a small blue star. Head props, pillows, and blankets, funny how pets, exactly like us, gravitate to such comforts. But on this steamy, 88-degree day in early July, Hannah looked comfortable; yet, accustomed to sharing the back seat with Orion, she also seemed somewhat pensive, or lonely.

She missed him. Slept more at home, wandered our house as if searching for her lively pal, and her appetite was still off. Generally, a happy dog—easy to be around, cooperative, fun-loving—Hannah was now an "only child," so to speak: Lola gone for more than a year, Orion, for only three months. We hadn't been a one-pet household since the Sidney days, and sadly, due to my allergies, another kitten wasn't an option. Even thinking about a new dog, a companion for Hannah, once again, was difficult.

"Hannah doing okay?" John asked, as I turned back around, glanced at a collection of highway signs. Traffic was sparse, but typical for a Sunday morning. "She must not like the scenery through here since she's hanging out in the back seat." We laughed, or tried to.

"She's nearly asleep," I said. "Strange, though, to see her alone." With a lingering sigh, I surveyed the summer sky. Appreciating a tranquil plane of blue with tufts of white and pale gray, I added, "But, you know, Orion never did like car rides."

Beginning without fanfare or unease, there wasn't the slightest hint of what was coming that blustery day in late March. Orion and Hannah, eager to spend time outside after a long winter of frigid temps, blowing snow, distant sunshine, had run off our deck in hot pursuit of a rabbit. Drifts hadn't cleared our yard yet, especially on the north, but they maneuvered their way around them with ease.

Watching them chase each other—ears flopping, stub tails wagging—I was happy they had each other. The days of Hannah being a "difficult decision" were long forgotten. They had bonded easily, despite Orion's alpha dog nature. Maybe her beguiling eyes got to him, too. She had the most intense stare when she wanted attention or a treat. I doubted that they missed Lola—dogs will be dogs—but then again, it's impossible to say with any certainty what sentiments or hidden longings have developed between animals that, over time, have grown attached to each other.

With a cold wind, a pale sun being swallowed by thick, fast-moving clouds, they raced back to the door—effortlessly navigating three slippery steps—before I could call them in. After big gulps of water, they settled down for a nap.

Orion preferred the couch; Hannah jumped in her round, red plaid bed. Almost too small, she curled up tight, then dozed off. Mid-afternoon, I went in the kitchen, found an apple. When they were up and about again, I'd offer them some small pieces—in the meantime, I enjoyed a few slices before returning to my computer.

When it came to apples, I was a Granny Smith fan, probably because of my grandmother's glorious apple trees. I'd loved those bountiful trees. Covered with sweet-smelling blossoms in spring, as kids, we eagerly watched the apples grow during the summer, often picking them before they were ripe and sprinkling them with salt. Countering the tart, sharp-on-the-tongue taste, to this day, salt and apples, for me, are an automatic pairing.

I have no idea what kind of apples my grandmother grew, but they weren't a red variety, and we never seemed to know (or care) when they were officially ripe. Her apples, trees never sprayed, featured an abundance of blemishes and worm holes; but, as carefree kids, we simply ate around the worrisome spots. If an apple looked especially damaged, we'd get out her cutting board, cut it in half, but by the time we removed the bad parts, most of the apple had disappeared.

Always generous with neighbor kids, Anna loved to wash and bag apples to give away. To this day, I can't eat an apple without these memories—sparkling threads in time—springing to mind.

JOHN HAD A BIRTHDAY COMING UP, so back at my computer, I thought I'd try some online shopping. Without a specific idea, I considered all the usual things: books, music, clothes, decadent cakes, candy, maybe salted caramels from Bissinger's in St. Louis. I even looked at casual shoes before opting to wait for a more inspired choice. Never a big fan of buying something merely because of calendar dictates, a form of mindlessly feeding our commercialistic culture, something would come to me.

Switching back to work, I opened a couple of documents, tried to tackle some new poems. But I'd felt strangely tired all day, and when the sugar from the apple didn't kick in, as hoped, and I couldn't shake my low-energy vibes, I surrendered. Gave up, turned off my desk lamp. Writers learn, at some point, that creative work can't be forced. Rather, it must be gently drawn from the very shadows of existence.

Maybe it's just the weather, exhaustion from a long winter. So I'd mused before resorting to a short nap, a few more pages in a book I'd started the week before. A memoir by Dani Shapiro, *Hourglass: Time, Memory, Marriage,* I'd followed her work for years. Always down-to-earth, yet insightful and searching, *Hourglass,* a book of only 145 pages with an elegant black-and-white cover photograph, had captured my interest from the first sentence. Marriage, *any marriage,* is a dual challenge of self-growth and effective relationship evolution; as Shapiro adroitly focuses on promises kept, promises broken, there are many thought-provoking passages in her book.

ONLY TWENTY MINUTES OUTSIDE New Ulm, we were approaching a town of 3,600 people called Sleepy Eye. Since driving on Minnesota highways, we'd encountered plenty of annoying safety features called "speed bumps" or "rough treads." Per Wikipedia, they originated in 1952 in New Jersey. Designed to wake up weary drivers near key intersections and prevent them from drifting too far to the side of the road, they are officially known as "rumble strips."

We didn't mind them; Hannah, however, was seriously unnerved by their harsh, grating rattle. Shaking uncontrollably, each time we drove over one, she jumped to the floorboard or into my lap; ears back, she'd tuck her head between my neck and shoulder as though frightened beyond recovery. Anxiety

Sleepy Eye and Linus

and trembling continued for miles, despite the reassurance we offered. And as you have likely surmised, just when she'd settled down, stopped quivering, yet another rumble strip, and off she'd go again. Stressful for many animals, I wonder if anyone thought about this piece of the puzzle before crews added them to highways across the country. Perhaps, however, they save lives; I hope so.

Much to Hannah's relief, we decided to stop for gas in Sleepy Eye. What a name for a town! Curious about its origins, while John filled the tank, I turned to my cell phone for an online explanation. Within seconds, I'd learned the small town dated back to 1872, when initially platted. Named after Chief Sleepy Eye, a Sioux Native American who played a role in land negotiations in southern Minnesota, it sits on US Highway 14 and MN 68.

Hannah had jumped to the back seat—travel worries momentarily forgotten—and was watching John from an open window. Panting happily, she was probably ready to find a nice patch of grass. We always traveled with a jar of ice water, so I poured some into her bowl. It wasn't until we were ready to get back on the highway that we spotted the library directly across the street.

"John, isn't that a statue of Linus—you know, the Charles Schultz Linus, the Orion *Linus* Tobias namesake?"

"Looks like it! Let's go find out. Hannah can check out the grass."

Once across the street, we realized the life-size statue was right in front of the Dyckman Free Library on 345 Main Street West. Gawking like tourists, we noticed Snoopy snoozing on the famous blue security blanket, with Linus clutching a red heart that says "I love Sleepy Eye." Piling out of the car, Hannah on her leash, we walked closer. Scanning donor plaques and historical information, we learned that "this Linus," made from hollow plastic, was 62 inches tall, 34 inches thick, and 45 inches at its base. A tribute to Linus Maurer, Sleepy Eye native and namesake for the beloved "Peanuts" character, Maurer met Charles Schultz while they were both teaching at the Minneapolis School of Art. Becoming lifelong friends, Maurer (1926–2016), later a California resident, designed puzzles and became an award-winning cartoonist, as well.

"Lovely tribute," I said, glancing at John—Hannah, waiting for whatever came next, sat nearby. "What are the odds of stumbling across this today? The magic of staying on Highway 14, I guess."

I couldn't help but think about O.

Like Linus, his insecure ways, and how we'd added Linus to his name before we even knew how apropos it was for him. His blue, Linus-like blanket, now Hannah's. And there were his early puppy days spent in Tracy, Minnesota—us back in Minnesota on our first road trip without him.

"Fun discovery," John said. "Bet it's an interesting old library too. We should come back when we have time to wander the dusty book aisles."

After walking Hannah around the grounds, we were back in the car. The realtor, meeting us at the house we planned to see in New Ulm, likely wouldn't be overjoyed if we were late. Still unsure about moving, with Noah, Lola, and now Orion gone, we craved a brighter view. New streets to drive on, new people to meet, but most of all, a place to lessen the hefty feelings of loss bottled up in our house like a litany of sad tales hiding behind the curtains, under the beds, and in our closets.

That early spring afternoon when I'd stood at the slider watching them dodge the remaining snow drifts, the sky refusing much light or warmth, was Orion's last good frolic with Hannah. Memories of that day rattled on as the last few miles ticked by.

LATE AFTERNOON, I'D PLAYED FETCH with Hannah, while Orion, still laying on the couch, watched. Unusual, but not a red flag. When Hannah was tired of running after her toys, apple pieces in hand, I worked with her on "come" and "sit" and "down." Again, Orion watched, but showed no interest in angling for a treat.

That's unusual, I thought, making a quick mental note to keep close tabs on him. Early evening rolled around. I pulled out their bowls, put the usual amount of food in Hannah's, but only a small amount in Orion's. He seemed so lackadaisical, so tired or *something,* I wondered if he would eat anything at all. John walked in a few minutes later, and by then, I'd realized Orion wasn't feeling well. Unwilling to even touch his food—a rare event—we assumed, not illogically, that his pancreatitis had worsened. He had medicine for his symptoms, so we dug it out, and hoped he would be better by morning.

As things turned out, a false hope. During the night he vomited, was low-energy in the morning, and by mid-morning had barely nibbled on his food.

During his 2016 pancreatic attacks, he'd suffered from severe diarrhea and vomiting that only could be stopped with a special injection. This time, nearly two years later, such signs were oddly missing; he didn't seem to be in pain, was mostly, tired. But the noticeable urgency in John's voice, when he brought Orion in from outside later in the day, got us moving.

Maybe 3:30 in the afternoon by then, we'd been closely monitoring his trips outside in case he was experiencing new or different symptoms.

"Blood in his urine," John said. "Call the vet, we need to go now."

Grabbing my jacket, I said, "I'll call on the way. Let's go."

Luckily, only minutes away, we were able to see someone right away. One of our favorite vets was available, but as he explained what Orion's symptoms might point to, I noticed the poorly disguised concern on his face.

"Where do we start?" I asked.

"Bloodwork," he replied. "We'll get it right over to the university, have results in an hour."

Moments later he returned with Orion. Labs had been drawn; they'd tried to get urine, as well, but due to discoloration, they weren't able to test it. Now we knew things were deadly serious. The myoglobin and hemoglobin in his urine that were making it red could damage his kidneys; the low oxygen-carrying capacity that can lead to liver damage, or shock, was a related concern. A complete blood count (CBC) and small-animal diagnostic profile revealed a low platelet count, and Orion's PCV (percentage of red blood cells circulating in blood) was also low, along with several other indicators. His PCV number pointed to red blood cell loss from cell destruction or something yet to be determined.

Orion's 104.3 temperature, his obvious lethargy, were more red flags. Our vet suspected possible IMHA (immune-mediated hemolytic anemia), which meant O's immune system was potentially destroying its own red blood cells. A Coombs test was needed to confirm this, however, and the local lab was closing for the weekend. *A Friday, of course.*

ITP (immune-mediated thrombocytopenia) was another possibility; it can occur with IMHA or separately. When both are present, symptoms are indicative of Evans Syndrome, an autoimmune disease that miniature schnauzers can be, according to some sources, more likely to experience. But Orion also needed an ultrasound.

We knew, by now, this was a full-fledged emergency, especially when our vet explained that dogs with such issues typically don't "last long" without immediate diagnosis and treatment.

Living in a small town of 18,000 residents, we knew none of these things were going to happen quickly. We discussed emergency care in Sioux Falls—forty-five miles south—but we had a higher comfort level with the University of Minnesota Veterinary Medical Center in Minneapolis (Noah's gall bladder surgery was done there). As soon as John could pack a bag for the four-hour trip, they would start out.

Orion was fading fast, and a late spring, ten-inch snowstorm was due within hours. Nightfall was almost upon us, as well. Orion had been on intravenous fluids while we worked on diagnosis and a plan of action; we hoped this would help him make the trip. Totally panicked, paperwork in hand, we hurried to our car, stopped for gas, and drove home.

Our minds raced, as we struggled to piece this all together. A frightening turn of events, Orion rested on my lap, eyes closed. Unaware of the danger, the fear, that already had lodged in our hearts, he had no way to know that we were in some form of shock. Unable to believe something had gone terribly wrong with so little warning, we felt like robots in crisis mode.

Pushing on, pushing through. Maybe the snowstorm will miss us; maybe O's life-threatening condition will respond to treatment. *Maybe they can save him.*

On the way home, I called the UMVMC emergency room to let them know Orion was coming in, and that I would be faxing the paperwork from our local vet within minutes. Luckily, Orion was in their computer system.

Less than two years ago, we'd consulted with an expert there about pancreatitis; when it came to prescription food, our options were limited. Mostly, we wanted to be sure we were doing everything possible to avoid additional attacks.

John threw his overnight bag in the car, as I gathered together some things for Orion: water, food, blanket, a couple of stuffed toys, his coat in case the snow was heavy. He didn't like to wear a warm coat, but humored us, nonetheless. We checked the forecast one more time. Nearly six o'clock, under good road conditions, they wouldn't be in Minneapolis until ten.

I wished them good luck, gave Orion some gentle strokes to reassure and comfort him, told him I loved him, that he'd be home again soon—dumb stuff, really. Crisis brain is a lot like morning brain; we speak from apprehension and fear, forgetting how unnecessary most words are in the moment.

His IV catheter was temporarily capped, taped to a front leg with blue Velcro. Lying on a blanket in the passenger seat, he looked worn out. Resigned to whatever fate awaited him. Believing this wasn't a final good-bye, I'd decided to stay home with Hannah. We'd had no time to arrange for her care (we didn't board our dogs, anyway), so it was the best we could do under the circumstances; but as I watched them drive away, a heavy jolt of fear and sadness hit me.

This was a very sick dog; treatment was complicated and odds weren't good that he would survive. Possible, but not probable, was my understanding. In reviewing the medical notes forwarded to the University, I'd spotted unfamiliar terms I wanted to research. Cholangiohepatitis, in particular. The intimidating term had been explained to us, but functioning under the debilitating influence of worry and fear, it's difficult, if not impossible, to listen closely.

The mind wanders, the heart flutters in a vain attempt to protect itself.

AFTER THEY LEFT, I immediately turned on the television to catch the weather for eastern travel into the twin cities. How was it that we were in line for ten inches of snow this late in the season—March 23, to be precise? If a strong wind came up, visibility would be treacherous, and a sick dog to care for en route would complicate things. *Life isn't fair* rattled through my thoughts, until Hannah jumped on my lap, studied my eyes as though she knew something was dreadfully wrong. Earlier, I'd spotted her in O's crate—looking for him, sniffing his toys, blankets.

"I know, Hannah," I said, "but he'll be back soon."

Who I was trying to reassure? Too soon to give up hope, part of me felt that bad news was inevitable. Intuition, partially, plus his slim odds for recovery.

We sat together for a while, until I tried to interest her in fetch, but she wasn't up for it. Hannah knew the routine had shifted. Something was up, caution was the word. But I knew exactly where she'd go. Waiting for John and Orion on the window seat made perfect sense: a place of comfort, security. And a place where she'd spent hours on end with Orion.

An hour later, she was still there—noticing every noise, gazing out the window, and waiting. Street lights illuminated snow coming down in heavy, swirling streams, but John had called, said he was thirty-some minutes ahead of the weather. The roads were still good.

"How's Orion?" I'd asked. "Sleeping?"

"We stopped briefly," he said. "But the wind is awful. It's cold. He peed, and that was it. I offered water, a bit of food, but no interest. He's definitely struggling."

"Did we do the right thing?" I imagined extensive medical intervention without good results. A prognosis no one wants to hear. "I don't want him to suffer," I said.

"We'll know more soon. Maybe it's not as bad as we are imagining. Maybe."

COMING OUT OF MY Orion reverie, I spotted the sign for New Ulm. Everything was summer green—promising, vital. The realtor had called to confirm time and place after our stop in Sleepy Eye; we only had about ten minutes to find the house. New Ulm, a town of 13,000 or so residents, is home to the long-running Schell Brewery.

Built in 1860 when German immigrant, August Schell, launched an enduring business, the company, one of the oldest family-owned breweries in the country, as you might expect, specializes in German-style lagers. We liked Goosetown, an ale. According to Schell's website, it's "golden orange" with a "light and citrusy tartness backed by a bready malt character and complimented with coriander spice."

As our speed slowed, Hannah landed in my lap. We appreciated her comforting presence more than common words can capture. Had my crystal ball been working—had we known Lola and Orion would follow Noah's final days in rather quick succession—we never would have hesitated, or wondered, about the wisdom of a third dog.

Noah, June 2015. Lola, May 2017. Orion, March 2018.

It wasn't getting any easier to lose them, either.

Still on my lap, Hannah stirred, like she'd read my thoughts, and despite the heat, I dropped my window for her. She stuck out her nose, sniffed the air.

"Hey, I think we're getting close," John said, driving by another city park. "We're a few minutes late, but not bad."

New Ulm was an award-winning community, and he'd been there before for work-related meetings. Situated near the Minnesota and Cottonwood Rivers, we thought it was one of the prettiest towns we'd ever driven through.

"I think I'd miss South Dakota," I said, quietly. "It's home, and the place where we met, got married."

My mother, as mentioned, had passed away in late 2017. Though in very poor health during her last years, she was one of the reasons we'd moved back to my home state from Indianapolis in 2008.

I'd written my first book about South Dakota in 1999. After revisiting the topic and sensing some updates would be useful, I published a second edition in 2014, under a new title: *Always Returning: The Wisdom of Place*. My roots, as they say, ran pretty deep, and given all the loss we'd endured since my son's tragic death in 2007, as we neared the house, I felt increasingly cautious, uncertain. A litany of reservations swirled and swiveled, irrespective of the sense of "new and different" we were aiming for in a town appropriately called New Ulm.

"I'd miss it, too," John said, as we caught a glimpse of a house on a hill with four deer grazing in the front yard. "That's it," he said. "Looks nice."

"Love the deer!"

Yes, of course, I should have known there would be deer. A message from nature that this was the spot. The house. The town. And the moment.

We spotted the realtor parked in the driveway, and suddenly, I felt badly for wasting his time. But, waving to him, I couldn't help but feel intrigued by the backyard which was essentially a small forest of green on a slope. Beautifully landscaped, it was truly picturesque: a tranquil reprieve. And we'd selected homes based on the backyard more than once. Living close to nature, a consistent priority for us.

Stepping from our vehicles, sweltering heat rising up around us, we introduced ourselves and asked if Hannah also could come in if we carried her. We'd stumbled across a dog-lover, so he was fine with that. A middle-aged man showing his years, he reached down, gave her a pat on the head after she sniffed his hand.

"We love dogs," he said. "It bothers me when I see dogs stuck in hot cars. I report it every time." But then he swiftly turned his attention back to the house; it wasn't new or modern, but in good repair. "The owners only live here briefly in the summer months. Snowbirds . . . retired," he added, with a smile. Handing us the listing with all the gory details, he mentioned that recently, the owners reduced the price. "It's bigger than some people want, and new construction has taken its toll."

Clearly, it wasn't a contemporary property, but three fireplaces helped, and the fantastic appliances (we loved to inhabit a pleasant kitchen, as you know) were a nice plus. We also appreciated all the glass to the west, the lovely patio, and the deck off the master bedroom. By the time we'd walked through the house, finished lower level included, we knew this was more space than two people and a small dog needed. No worries about having enough room for two home offices.

Walls covered in a floral wallpaper didn't appeal to us, and the kitchen was on the small side, yet, to be fair, the house had character, personality. *And the deer in the front yard.* But as we thanked the realtor for his time, John and I knew it wasn't "the" house. Like the past itself, it felt like a nice home from a tired yesterday; and the massive yard, though offering considerable privacy, solitude for writing, and the luxury of space to enjoy nature, was clearly a great deal of work.

As we drove away, I said, "Fun to see it, at least. He was nice. Knowledgeable."

John agreed, but within seconds we were talking about lunch—what restaurant we wanted to try in New Ulm. We couldn't go inside because of Hannah, so we thought it might be best to pick up something and find a nice park.

"Let's find Main," John suggested. "I remember some of the restaurants from earlier trips. Not by name, but I'll recognize them."

Seems like our lunch consisted of sauerkraut balls from Veigel's Kaiserhoff. We also had crispy battered green beans, bratwurst and hot German potato salad, but passed on the bread pudding with raisins and lemon sauce. After driving by several city parks, we opted for one with towering and abundant shade trees.

Talking about the town, the German food, the house and deer, an hour later, we said good-bye to New Ulm. Driving west on Highway 14, as we hit the city limits, I recalled a few words from my first book: *Quite often, the prairie's everlasting beauty is best found in the eye of the beholder.* The prairie I grew up with definitely wasn't for everyone—vast open spaces, towering blue skies, the seldom tree—but for now, at least for us, it was home.

Twenty-three

TENDER MOMENTS

Traveling home from New Ulm, I was soon lulled to sleep by the hypnotic highway, the motion, the thoughts sailing through my head. Good thing John had offered to drive. But nearing the small town of Walnut Grove, he nudged me.

"Want to stop?" he asked. "A popular Laura Ingalls Wilder tourist spot."

"Sure," I mumbled. "We should. I loved her books."

"I've been thinking about Orion," he said. "Linus in Sleepy Eye, and driving by the place where I picked him up as a puppy that cold, dark afternoon in January—vivid memories. I miss that guy."

"On my mind today, too," I said, still sleepy, relaxed. "Were we hoping to escape history by moving?"

"Are we that smart?" His question got a laugh out of us. "Escape or not, it's been a nice day. And I didn't have to mow or water the trees."

"New Ulm, realistically, could have been a nice place to live had we decided to push ourselves in that direction." John nodded, commented on the house again—the biggest draw, deer in the front yard.

Almost in Walnut Grove, Hannah was eyeing my lap again, so I invited her up. "She's all girl," I said. Unlike Noah and Orion, she didn't destroy her toys (not even in her wild puppy days), merely shook them around for dear life. Crunching hidden squeakers to create "music" appealed to her, as well.

Our male dogs, conversely, took after toys with zeal. Seriously intent on "killing" them—biting and chewing until they pierced the fabric to extract the horrible manmade stuffing—their toys, sadly, had a short life span.

Hannah was also noticeably sensitive to human emotion—when she saw tears, she rushed over to offer comfort—and if my voice grew firm, due to possible danger, i.e., a hot oven door, or whatever, she listened closely. Sensing fear, as in the midst of Orion's crisis, she jumped in my lap, gazed into my eyes—brown eyes wide, intense, curious—or with back paws on the floor, front paws on my lap, she'd stare up at me with an intense energy. A star member of our no worries club, she had been an extremely fortuitous decision.

"Here we are," John said, pulling off the highway. "Let's go get inspired by Laura Ingalls Wilder. Or at least we can fake it, right?"

"Is this like the Wilder homestead in De Smet, South Dakota? Remember that place, west of us by twenty minutes or so, the tour we took one summer?"

"We'll have to find out," John said. "Don't know her bio that well, except that her pioneer family moved a lot."

The late afternoon sun still beating down, we spotted a covered wagon in the distance, along with a building that looked like a small museum. Tourists milled around the grounds, but it wasn't crowded. We found a parking place with a hint of shade, then looked around for a "no dogs allowed" sign. Or a "dogs must be leashed" sign. Hoping the management was "dog friendly," we wanted to let Hannah out for a little break, but we didn't see any helpful clues.

"I'll go ask about Hannah," John said. "Water, ice tea, candy bar, chips?"

John's weakness, potato chips—any flavor, any style—but hot and spicy, or barbeque, were the usual suspects.

"Water, sure."

Parked in front of a historical sign, I learned more about the well-known author while he was inside. Living, from 1874 to 1876, north of Walnut Grove by 1.5 miles along the banks of Plum Creek, I instantly remembered her book, *Plum Creek*, as I read. But due to crop failures, family plans to homestead there hadn't panned out, so lacking options in those days, they packed up, moved to Burr Oak, Iowa. Her family also lived in Kansas for a time; their homesteading days in Dakota Territory began in 1879.

During their Walnut Grove years, they all lived in a pioneer "dugout home." The actual site—now, only a deep depression in the land—featured twenty-five acres of native prairie grasses. After Laura got married, she remained in South Dakota for several years enduring a string of hardships, until moving to Missouri with Almanzo Wilder, her husband, in 1894. *Almanzo, from her books, a familiar name.* Laura (1867–1957), born in Wisconsin, died in Mansfield, Missouri.

A small, unassuming town in the Ozarks of south-central Missouri, where she wrote the Little House books by hand, their Rocky Ridge Farm is a popular tourist attraction with an impressive calendar of events.

Hannah barked, she'd spotted John.

"We can walk Hannah on a leash," he said, "but the museum is off-limits."

He handed me the water, and Hannah, panting, despite our air conditioned car, looked at me, then at John, like "well, let's get out. What are we waiting for?"

John got her leash, and like tourists, we strolled around the grounds until the heat got to us. I offered to drive the last leg of our trip home, so he could nap this time. As we drove away, he opened a rather large bag of potato chips from the gift shop. "Barbeque, want a couple?"

"Just one," I said, adjusting my seat and mirrors. I liked chips, but it was one salty temptation I could nearly always resist. "Read about Wilder's history while you were in there, we'll have to visit Mansfield, Missouri, sometime."

As THE MILES TICKED BY, the sky filled with late-afternoon clouds. Three months ago, John had been on this same highway on his way to Minneapolis with O.

When they arrived, parked, emerged from the car, he said Orion walked right in like he felt fine. We'd gotten our hopes up, of course. Amazing how tough our little guy was, given his health. They beat the snow, but the storm followed them. Heavy snow, biting winds, letting loose less than an hour after Orion was admitted as an emergency patient.

We felt very fortunate to have the resources to take Orion to the University of Minnesota Veterinarian Medical Center. At a young six and a half years, he deserved another chance. Of course that was probably the wrong way to look at life and time: united like the best, the worst, of friends.

No guarantees. No magical extensions. A harsh indifference to hard-luck stories.

John had kept me well-informed, sending pictures of Orion and reports from the emergency room doctors, but the prognosis was never encouraging. Struggling with an extremely serious auto-immune problem, the source, never determined, Orion, despite wonderful care, couldn't seem to rally.

John and Hannah had fallen asleep, traffic was light. Our conversations from that stressful time drifted through my thoughts.

"More diagnostics planned for tomorrow," he said. "Since he's hospitalized, would you believe, there are formal visiting hours?"

"Hopefully, they're flexible," I'd said, imagining O stuck in a crate in a foreign, possibly frightening, environment. "Do they think this is connected to pancreatitis? Can they at least stabilize him?"

"No new information, maybe tomorrow. Hated to leave him there, though. You know how he is."

"They're giving him pain meds, keeping him comfortable, right?"

"Right," John said, in a tone of voice that, sadly, foreshadowed the days ahead.

By the next morning we had ten inches of snow, and Orion was not getting any better. They were talking about blood transfusions. We hesitated. But even against the odds, we hoped he might pull through—at a minimum, intervention might aid research to help other animals—so reluctantly, we followed their recommendations.

Worried that Orion was suffering—lethargic, no appetite, IVs, and surrounded by strangers—we finally called a vet (and a friend) who usually offered great advice. Reassuring us that animals with auto-immune problems *can* pull through, we still struggled to stay even reasonably optimistic.

Unable to see Orion made me even more uneasy. Our imaginations run wild at times like this. Waiting, from afar, for a shred of good news to trickle in, I was restless, paced anxiously, and avoided looking at his crate.

They tried a blood transfusion without noticeable results, and, soon thereafter, a second one that we were very uncertain about authorizing. Hospitalized for three days without tangible results, Orion's care—a long shot at best—was becoming an investment, and our emotions were taut, starting to fray.

But, surprisingly, by Monday evening—they'd arrived Friday night—our sweet dog perked up. The excitement in John's voice was so good to hear.

"He even tried to play a little when I took him outside just now. A small thing, but maybe he can pull through somehow."

"That's great," I said, before catching myself. "Say he does make it, but maybe it's Evan's Disease or something else that's chronic, incurable, requiring intensive follow-up care. Do we *really* want to put him through that?" I also felt like we were getting our hopes up in a seriously naive kind of way. "I read this afternoon that he would need drug therapy with consistent monitoring for the rest of his days. A real roller coaster."

We both sighed with the strain of not knowing—the emotional weight of harsh realities.

"Sad to think his body is attacking itself. Certain infectious tick bites can trigger problems like this, but there aren't any ticks out yet. *It's still winter.* Frustrating." Pausing, John added, "I'll text O's picture before I leave here tonight. He's still not eating, has a nasal tube now too."

"Oh no," I said, my voice a worried whisper. "Another tube, poor guy."

"Orion can't be enjoying any of this. Looks tired, sad, confused. When I leave, he gives me that frightened, desperate aren't-you-staying-with-me look."

The picture he sent was sobering.

Resting on John's outstretched legs in a small, impersonal visiting cubicle, Orion wore a standard white hospital band around his neck. Due to IVs, two or three legs were partially wrapped. Ears and head were low, and overall, he looked fatigued. I wanted to comfort him, pet him—his coat, usually shiny, looked dull, flattened—and touch his ears. How they used to perk up when he heard my voice.

When upset, frightened, or avoiding a bath, Orion made a beeline to me. Though he could seem gruff when excited, unsure, or threatened, O had a true soft side. And his incredible hearing. Not even a gust of wind slipped by him.

Canine hearing, as I later learned, is four times as sensitive as humans; it also includes an ability to hear at higher frequencies. And their ears are so expressive, moving up and down, back and forth, because they have some eighteen muscles in their earflaps.

Just imagine having such sensitive hearing when an intolerant, irritated human being yells or rages at you.

UP EARLY THE NEXT MORNING, I'd bravely hoped for an optimistic report that could lead to his recovery—a chance to bring Orion home. Coffee made, I opened the door for Hannah, surveyed all the wet snow that hadn't melted yet; it was sad watching her meander around our backyard. She looked lost without her sidekick, and her white coat, seamlessly blending with the snow into a blanket of white, made O's absence—his thick, sky-black coat—even more glaring.

I wondered what this poignant scene might portend. Was it a harbinger of loss? Was Orion's destiny clear? Were we unable to see it, believe it?

"C'mon, Hannah," I called from the doorway. Looking my way, she raced up the slushy stairs, ran inside where I attempted to pry clinging snowballs from her legs and feet. Mostly impossible, Hannah patiently waited for me to give up. "Good girl," I said, stroking her head.

Moments later, a brief text.

"I'll call soon. O's kidneys have failed. Talking to doctors."

Looking down, I closed my eyes to contain instant tears. This was the end—a point of no return.

"Nothing they can do for him now," John explained minutes later. "Took him outside this morning, and he sat down, eyes tired, blank."

It's hard to hear your husband cry.

Orion had been *his* dog. The love, the trust, between them was joyful, real.

Our sweet Orion died on a Tuesday. John's birthday, only two days later. How was that fair? How was this even happening? And, of course, I cried. And cried. Hannah trailed me around the house, staring with saucer-shaped eyes, as though begging me to *please* explain what was wrong.

As I slowed for the next town, John stirred, so I whispered, "We're almost home, near Tracy." I knew he'd want to see the small Minnesota town that was Orion's first home, the large horse barn outside of town with a beautiful black schnauzer painted on a white slopping roof.

The western sun was blinding at this point, so he shielded his eyes, looked for his sunglasses. "Driving west is no damn picnic this time of day."

Moments later, we glanced off to the left, and there it was. I think we sighed in unison. Memories of our joyful, energetic Orion rushing to the fore.

"When I pulled up that super cold day, I heard the schnauzers barking. I'll never forget meeting Orion—ran straight over to me like he'd been waiting for *me* to show up. Those pleading eyes, last of his litter, he wanted his turn at a good home. With his eager demeanor, I knew he'd be a handful—but one we'd love."

Hannah, head out the window, panting happily, sniffed the summer air. And as we drove past O's first home, she barked. John and I looked at each other and tears erupted. A nod to Orion from Hannah was more than we could take. We knew our grief-stricken imaginations were working overtime, but logic was useless.

Besides, I've long believed that seemingly unlikely moments—uncanny, deeply poignant, surreal—beyond time and place, are connected to hidden energy fields, concealed dimensions. And for whatever reason, Hannah's solitary bark—urgent, insistent—felt as real as all the love we'd ever known for Orion.

In that moment, our small black-and-silver dog, his commanding bark protecting a shy heart, with the flashy eyebrows—pal and playmate to Noah and Hannah, and cautious chum to Lola—traveled west with us as an intense July sun inched lower with every mile.

Twenty-four

THE STILL POINT

Settling back into our work routines in the following weeks took some effort. But I'd starting working on this book about a month before Orion's sudden loss, so I knew I had to face the blank page eventually. Wholeheartedly, instead of reluctantly. After Orion's one-way trip to Minneapolis, my commitment, like a freight train slowing to a stop, whined and sputtered. Overwhelmed by the intensity of writing—emotions I'd be forced to face along the way—I could only wonder why I ever wanted to write this book in the first place.

Naively or optimistically, I'd believed Orion was our "last dog," then I was sure Hannah was our "last dog." Yet, change—uninvited, resisted, grieved—had strolled into my life on an ordinary day, and the chapter about Sleepy Eye and Linus, one never envisioned, became a reality anyway.

Hannah, not without nicknames of her own—Hanner, Hanne, Hannah Banana, HanRose, when we added her middle name—seemed to sense my ongoing struggle to resume a story

I'd been really excited about working on until things took a sad, unexpected turn. Lying by my feet to nap, shadowing my every move, she looked at me with her big, receptive eyes—a touch of longing tucked around the edges.

"Oh, sweet Hannah," I'd say, while she wagged her tail, pricked her ears. "Like the tart crust I hid in the freezer when O's early symptoms surfaced, at some point, we must face the dawn. Get the crust out of the freezer, finish the recipe. Or, write the next word. The story . . . must go on."

Listening closely, I knew she was waiting to hear one of her favorite words: treat, fetch, walk, let's go, good girl, John's home, go see.

The crust idled in the freezer until November—a good six months after I'd baked it that gentle spring day in early May. Rummaging through mountains of collected, but poorly organized, recipes, the bittersweet-chocolate tart recipe was lost between past and present. Finally spotting it, the sharp sting of remembering swooped in.

Orion, eventually diagnosed July of 2016 with pancreatitis, or something very much like it, would never be free from serious health issues. Realistically, health is always imperfect, but having lost Noah only a year prior, the days ahead felt especially fragile.

His condition might worsen. We could lose him, too. And sweet Lola, at fifteen, how much longer did she have?

Brushing instinctive worries aside, I'd measured out cream, milk, cocoa powder, sugar, and bittersweet chocolate. The recipe also called for two eggs, plus a small amount of gelatin; but the recipe didn't seem nearly as daunting as remembered, and, luckily, it all came together nicely that day.

Finally, settling into my office, coffee nearby, I opened the book document called *Happy Truth*. It didn't take long to read and edit the last chapter I'd written, but finding a path to the next one was a significant hurdle. For nonwriters, it may seem impossible to imagine, but a book-in-progress epitomizes a cold, rocky, almost always inhospitable terrain; and like creative artists the world over, I was clinging to a sketchy map that lurked in shifting shadows.

Then, like a sudden breeze, the light came on when I remembered I was making this more difficult than necessary—when I remembered that everything flows from silence. Glancing at Hannah, snoozing in her bed less than three feet from my desk, one of O's old toys, a hedgehog with black, beady eyes, tucked beside her, I let go of swirling thoughts and intimidating goals. Like settling into meditation, there was plenty of back and forth, until I squirmed free of incessant mind chatter.

Then, from a buoyant silence, something ridiculous crossed my mind: *a puppy*.

We'd talked about it once or twice since late March. Primarily, in jest. An idea that sounded logical, yet, totally illogical. Something that sounded vaguely wrong, almost dreamlike, in the face of Orion's brief life. Nonetheless, there it was, a single word coming to me from the expansive, quiet space I'd sought to summons a bridge to the next chapter. Open that hallowed door and one never knows what will fall through, become fully conscious, or newly visible.

A puppy. Hannah needs a new friend; she misses Orion.

My book, barely in the initial stages, had yet to be written; this "puppy idea" wasn't what I went looking for in terms of picking up the narrative after a long absence. But, T.S. Eliot, in the poem, "Burnt Norton," the first of his *Four Quartets,* must have known something deeply important when he wrote: "At the still point, there the dance is."

Publishing *Four Quartets,* celebrated meditations exploring humanity's complex relationship to time, the universe, and the divine, over a span of six years, Eliot's achievement was deemed a literary feat by many. Likening the project to weaving four superficially dissimilar poems into a connected whole, the famous work was a synthesis of ideas, if you will.

WE'D SERVED THE DELICIOUS bittersweet chocolate tart with whipped cream for dessert. The crust tasted fine, despite its stay in our freezer, and it spurred us on somehow with hopeful sentiments. That year, on November 18, Orion had turned five, only days before Thanksgiving.

Back to his spunky, high-spirited self, he looked pain-free and alert. Hannah, a year-plus by then, was still our "fetching queen." Jetting off in pursuit of any toy we tossed her way, never looking indifferent or bored, she loved the happy chase, the adrenalin rush; and precious Lola, proudly and calmly coping with advanced years, simply purred on.

That was then.

It was a new world without Noah, Orion, or Lola.

Of course Hannah needed a buddy of her own. I just hadn't ventured down that path until the unsought idea crept into my awareness. Gently so. Before I could resist or even dismiss it. Expecting to feel that old pull of worry and indecisiveness, like I had after Noah died and Hannah was also "just an idea," I didn't.

Only a faint flicker of resistance surfaced, then vanished. Had I finally graduated, made my way into the no worries club, the exclusive group that Sidney, Lola, Noah, Orion, and Hannah had created right before our eyes? Sleeping in positions that suggest *total* relaxation, gazing peacefully, as if contemplating the cosmos, or contentedly resting near us, all of our beautiful "pet kids" (kidlets?), cats and dogs alike, have radiated a soothing, seriously contagious, no worries vibe.

All along, have our cats and dogs—*mine and yours*—been leading the way?

"Hannah," I said, her head up and tipped to one side already, "let's go for a walk. What are we doing sitting in the house on this beautiful summer day in July?"

Rising to her feet, quickly coming over to me, she'd heard the word "walk," and nothing more was needed. Within minutes we were out the door and headed up to McCrory Gardens, our uplifting hideaway—birds, trees, water fountains, flowering shrubs, vines, native plants and prairie grass, and walking paths that wandered in no particular direction at all—right in the middle of town.

Nearing the Gardens, turning in, Hannah's quiet demeanor switched from "this is okay" to "this is great." She knew this place, loved it.

We parked in the shade, left a window cracked, and emerged from the car, water in hand. Aspen trees, tall, swaying in a light breeze, nearly surrounded us, and off in the distance, we spotted a couple walking by the informal rose garden.

Butterflies in an array of shapes and colors drifted lazily through the languid air, pausing briefly on zinnias and coneflowers and marigolds. Soon airborne again, I watched them glide amidst weightless puffs of cotton set free by giant cottonwood trees.

"All in all, it was a never to be forgotten summer," as author L. M. Montgomery wrote in *Anne's House of Dreams* in 1917.

Heading down a familiar path to the north, I could almost sense Orion and Noah trailing us, maybe even Lola. *Maybe* the puppy that was still "just an idea."

ON THE WAY HOME I thought about stopping for coffee at Kool Beans, a new place in town. A local company that had slowly gained popularity by coming to the Farmer's Market every Saturday morning between May and October, the ambitious owner had recently opened a storefront on Main. Roasting the coffee beans on-site, he also sold them in the store along with gluten-free breads and cookies. Kool Beans had really taken off, and a second location, fairly close to campus (South Dakota State University), was in the works. A drive-thru on sixth street, the busiest street in town and a direct connection to the interstate, the new location would be right across the street from McDonald's. That could only help.

But glancing over at Hannah, happily panting and looking out an open window, I decided to visit Kool Beans another time. We never took a chance leaving our dogs in the car when the temperatures weren't perfectly mild and safe.

Driving down Medary, toward Orchard, I wondered where we might find another puppy. How long would it take? Where would I begin our search this time?

Twenty-five

RING THEM BELLS

The world is full of good things and good people. Heartwarming stories abound. Love and courage exist. We *know* how to do the right thing. Take, for instance, a new program called "Calming Companions" initiated in Phoenix by the Maricopa County Animal Care and Control staff. Dogs or cats are often frightened by Fourth of July celebrations, human-style, so this innovative, inspirational program, invites volunteers into their shelters to sit with confined animals without homes. Life can be about "them," right? Doesn't always have to be about "us."

And guess what? Some 200 people showed up to sit with stressed animals living in crowded, impersonal conditions with abrasive fireworks fueling their tension and fear. Toting blankets and chairs to sit near kennels, some people played music, sang and talked to scared animals. Others read out loud or offered treats provided by the shelter. Leadership at its finest—Maricopa County, the volunteers who stepped up. I love it when we venture out on a shaky ledge to make a positive difference; when we have the vision to see beyond a problem and stare it down, finding ways to meet it head-on. Unfortunate animals existing in cramped, lonely shelters, may always be with us, but why not ease their trauma and anxiety, reach out when possible?

Sometimes it's the small acts of kindness—perceptive moments of noticing the suffering of other people and/or animals—that propel humanity forward. Though we may falter, our steps unsteady, seemingly of little consequence, when our hearts lead the way, beautiful things can happen. It's all about looking through the eyes of others, learning how to see the world with greater awareness and clarity.

Look closely at the animals in your home, or the ones you encounter otherwise, and notice how carefully they study their surroundings. They seem more grounded than humans, don't they? More observant. More content. Tapping powerful senses, they tune in to everything and everyone around them—they see before we see. And, perhaps, they see us more accurately than we see ourselves.

If you don't want to be seen—really seen—prefer to hide behind a fancy mask, an artificial persona crafted to your liking, animals, cats or dogs, in particular, may not be right for you. Because for them, *looking is seeing*. Looking is learning.

Conversely, we look, but don't always see. Or we look selectively, with minimal energy or interest, quickly rejecting what is uncomfortable, painful, threatening. Yet, the ability to perceive and acknowledge a more complete, painfully accurate, picture is imperative to human survival. Merely gleaning the bits and pieces that please or intrigue us isn't enough, I'm afraid.

Because of Sidney, Noah, Lola, Orion, and then, Hannah, we encountered life and death realities, challenging points of decision, moments of tremendous joy and sorrow. And we learned to look at life through their eyes—*penetrating windows to the world*—as we shared a multitude of sunny mornings, overcast afternoons, and stormy evenings with them.

Who is the teacher, the student?

Envisioning people of all ages and backgrounds sitting on blankets, cushions, portable chairs outside the metal confines of dog kennels on the Fourth of July, I also sensed another story of freedom lurking there. Perhaps a story even bigger than America's independence.

When, after all, are we the freest?

Might it be—*might it be*—when we look deeply and honestly at ourselves and the world around us, as if for the first time?

Again, I'm drawn to the luminous T.S. Eliot.

"Little Gidding," the last of Eliot's *Four Quartets,* contained these lovely lines: "We shall not cease from exploration, and the end of all our exploring will be to arrive where we started and know the place for the first time."

AS THE NOTION OF A PUPPY began to set in, summer wore on: hot and steady, wind and sporadic rain. Hannah kept things lively, falling into the "only child" role one day at a time. For the first time, she had our undivided attention. Orion had returned to us in a small wooden box with a return address of Pets Remembered, New Brighton, Minnesota—just minutes from Minneapolis.

Gingerly exploring the contents, we found a packet of seeds for Forget-Me-Nots, a brochure describing their services, website and social media links, information about their pet tribute service (please send pet photo with a tribute to share on their website, on Facebook), a sympathy card, an article about the many myths of grief by Alan Wolfelt, Ph.D., a memorial card noting a contribution in memory of Orion to a worthwhile organization called *Can Do Canines Assistance Dogs* at can-do-canines.org. There was even a Certificate of Cremation dated March 27, 2018.

The hardest thing to look at, though, was Orion's stamped footprint and a small clipping of fur, held together by a tiny piece of ribbon. Tucked in a "positively green" card with butterflies and a white flower, I read sentiments from Elizabeth Browne: "What the heart remembers most are memories shared."

All of this arrived in a burlap bag decorated with a reassuring rainbow and words of comfort. Engraved flowers on the small wooden box were "nice," yes, but somehow disquieting. There is really no way to make death into something it isn't—no way to "dress it up," so it's more tolerable, less traumatic. Sometimes well-meaning efforts backfire, in fact, but I was glad this professional business existed; I was grateful that a beloved animal was treated with regard. And that's far from inconsequential.

Looking over these items not long ago, I found Orion's six-inch blue and brown owl, a toy that, without fail, calmed him—one he'd carried around the house for months. Showing some wear, the stuffed toy had pink-and-brown eyes, long, floppy wings, stubby white feet (one missing), and still emitted plaintive hoots when squeezed. We've never been able to find another one, though we've looked.

I also ran across a sweet note from Steph, Orion's groomer. She'd sent flowers with a card that read: "Orion. Many sweet memories of his shy and tender heart run through my mind every time I see his name."

When I saw "his shy and tender heart," I knew she really understood and loved our little guy. Like the owl he loved to play with, Orion related to the world in his very own way.

BUT, AS I WAS SAYING, the world is full of good and kind-hearted people. Those who comfort fearful dogs on the Fourth of July. Those, like Linda P. Case, who writes insightful articles for "Whole Dog Journal: Your Complete Guide to Natural Dog Care and Training."

We loved this worthwhile publication.

Her article, "Comfort Your Dog," explained the fallacies of a persistent old myth that comforting your dog when he's frightened or anxious reinforces his fear.

Rather, it's the exact opposite.

We've learned, for instance, how calming music works miracles. Animals also show reduced signs of stress when human touch is safe and non-threatening, when we speak softly (remember, they hear much better than we do) and reassuringly to them. *When we are kind, genuine, caring.*

As Case, author of a new book, *Dog Smart,* notes in her article, "Fear/anxiety is not a choice." She explains that we should "calmly and quietly come to the dog's aid" when looking for an effective and humane way to respond to their anxiety. She also notes, trying to ignore a dog's stress is a "misguided attempt to change behavior."

So maybe we should keep in mind that the need for comfort and support isn't the sole domain of sometimes selfish, sometimes ill-informed, and sometimes downright heartless human beings. In fairness, the human species is also extremely capable of redemption, powerful caring, and selfless giving.

Possibly about the same time the word "puppy" sprang to mind from the silence I'd courted to get my book project moving again after losing Orion, another litter of schnauzers was being born (or whelped). Born, in fact, in July, on the *same day* as Hannah, and, once again, one, *only one* female in the litter. Not from the fun Star Wars clan, Hannah's "family," or a white puppy, the new female looked wonderfully unique.

In "parti colors" of white, tan, gray, and splashes of black, her colors struck me as artistic and ironic—the combined colors of all of our pets. A bringing together of various threads into a cohesive whole, like T.S. Eliot's vision for his *Four Quartets*.

If we followed through, she'd also be our fourth schnauzer.

We felt Hannah would do better with another female, so one sunny afternoon, she hopped in the back seat, and we drove off to see the puppies. If she approved, that would be another small sign, perhaps.

Already certain I would like her, John wondered if we wanted a "parti girl," and what was a "parti schnauzer," anyway.

"From what I've gathered," I explained, "the primary background color, white, is scattered with random spots of black, chocolate, salt and pepper. Or, maybe it's the other way around. White on a base color."

"But, in this case, she's gray, tan, white, with a touch of black?"

"I'm guessing salt and pepper against plenty of white when she matures. If she has more of a blended color, that's called ticking, I think. Intertwined shades that still contrast nicely with white. I didn't know this, but parti-patterned schnauzers have been around since the 1800s in Germany, but nearly became extinct."

"So they're making a comeback?" John asked. "You know I don't care about her color. Just wouldn't want her to look too much like Orion. Not ready for that."

I agreed, explaining that she looked like a magical blend of our other dogs. A coming together of the past. A new day. Of course, we also talked about the demands of a puppy, how we'd navigate the first year—second and third years, also puppy-like in many ways.

"Labor-intensive, but," John paused, "meaningful work, right?"

We laughed at that, Hannah leaning up between us as though eager to see the puppies, too. But, surprisingly, when we arrived, let her look them over, she was blatantly disinterested. A nearby patch of grass and a roving adult dog did get her attention, though. The really interesting part of our visit was that some three years later, she instantly remembered her breeder. Walked right over, tail wagging. A reunion that was a true pleasure to witness.

Peering in at squirming puppies, I saw the female, her unique colors standing out in the group. Gently picking her up, I let Hannah take a look. Again, no interest, but Lexy thought this was a good sign. Clearly, Hannah wasn't threatened or worried about the tiny fur ball in my hands. John took a turn holding her, and as you've already guessed, we loved her, already.

Finally, we let her join her male littermates again.

They all snuggled up in a corner, but within seconds, the little female emerged from the pack toting a tiny chew toy in nearly invisible teeth. When I spoke to her, she even barked. That was surprising! A tiny bark, given her age and size—five weeks, three pounds, if that—but we laughed at her spunk, nonetheless. *Maybe she likes us. Maybe she's trying to say: pick me.*

The other puppies, black and white mostly, and also very high on the cute scale, were completely oblivious to us.

Admittedly, right before her courageous woof, a spark of indecision had welled up, as I let my mind stumble down the rocky path of "what if," but who could ignore *that?* Didn't it pretty much seal the deal?

"When can we pick her up?" I ventured, sensing she had already chosen us.

We agreed to pick her up three weeks later, at eight weeks. On the drive down, we'd decided to name her Georgia, mostly because of the old song, "Georgia on My Mind." A 1930 jazz tune composed by Hoagy Carmichael and Stuart Gorrell (lyrics), many artists have recorded it, but Ray Charles is often linked to the song. On his 1960 album, *The Genius Hits the Road,* he took the beautiful song to new heights.

We also liked another well-known tune: "Midnight Train to Georgia," a 1973 hit by Gladys Knight and the Pips.

And didn't "Georgia" fit her somehow?

The sassy bark, her efforts to connect? Intent on chewing on a toy at five weeks, as though trying to impress us, was really pretty good, wasn't it?

Driving home, to avoid overlooking a better one, we batted around more names for our little "parti girl," but, in the end, we landed on Georgia Bliss O'Henri as her registered name.

In hindsight, Blaze would have been a better middle name for her, or Bell.

Blaze, because she would soon be racing around our house in those high-energy puppy ways. A fun term for this is "zoomies." Short for Frenetic Random Activity Periods (FRAPS), a "totally normal release of pent up energy," they last briefly and arise without warning. Very entertaining, I might add.

Bell, because we would survive Georgia's house-training months with bells on our doors, so she could ring them to get our attention when she had to go outside. She loved those bells, *still does*. Sometimes when she rings them, she merely wants to go out and play, and that's okay, too.

O'Henri is a combination of ideas.

As I shared earlier, John's beloved Henry Dog—stuffed, brown, oversized, and apparently, comforting to a young boy of long ago—gave us Henri. We opted for the female spelling of Henry, of course. The O, a special nod to the stars above, namely, Orion. Thus, O'Henri.

Why all of this thought for her name?

Because Georgia wasn't "just a dog" to us. She was fourth of four, and definitely, our "last dog." That's what we say, anyway. If T.S. Eliot was right, "four" makes a whole; but instead of *Four Quartets,* we had *Four Schnauzers* and *Two White Cats,* as a bonus, and what an immensely beneficial—sometimes challenging, yet always heartfelt—journey we've shared with them.

We've loved them all—each one brought special, beautifully unique gifts to our life and home. Each one helped us tap our finer instincts. Teacher, student? These roles are dynamic, fluid. When we are flexible—when we persistently seek personal growth—it's virtually impossible not to learn from the animals we love.

SINCE GEORGIA TOOK TO THE "bell training system" with enthusiasm, we often say to her, "ring them bells, G." The idea came from Bob Dylan; he recorded "Ring Them Bells" in 1989. One of those songs you never forget, it was the fourth tune on his *Oh Mercy* album. I can't recall many of the lyrics or what they were supposed to mean, but the melody itself is memorable.

Within weeks of bringing her home, the nicknames were flowing.

Like "O," I liked the brevity of one letter, so "G" came first, then Georgie, G-girl, G-bird (she was so petite), Gee-whiz, and G-bell.

WHEN WE PICKED HER UP, we didn't bring Hannah, but let them meet in a neutral location, as many experts recommend. Worked beautifully. Without a home base to defend, Hannah was relaxed and playful, and after sniffing, touching noses, and checking out each other, they immediately bonded.

"Sisters," someone wrote to me in a text.

We'd gone from never having a female, to having two females; so yes, we would probably think of them as sisters, especially since both were born on July 16.

That afternoon, sitting with them under a large oak in early September of 2018 at the Gardens where all of our dogs loved to walk, Georgia, tired from all of the activity, laid down on a blanket, closed her eyes. Before long Hannah joined her. Less than six months since we'd said good-bye to Orion, yet, we'd learned not to hold back. *Love and live while you can.*

Calendars and clocks aren't the answer. Time is fickle, and easily conceals the absolute brevity of our lives. So find your bliss, follow it faithfully, as the wonderfully wise author, mythologist, and professor Joseph Campbell implored.

And now you know the inspiration behind Bliss, Georgia's middle name. A good reminder—a timeless piece of advice—after we drove home, took her inside, there were moments of bliss. Along with plenty of hectic moments as Georgia flew around our house exploring every corner, her initial shyness suddenly overcome. At four or so pounds, compared to Hannah's twenty, she was still pretty fearless—except for stairs, loud noises, or being left alone.

Hannah studied her with calm curiosity and apparent goodwill.

The day had gone well, but we were all tired. Settling in would take a few days, but once we established a routine for her, things would evolve naturally. For now, Georgia had a new home; Hannah had a "sister." And our blissful dog quartet was complete. Not all at once, but over time.

Knowing Georgia would be up early, if not several times during the night, we tucked her in a padded crate in our bedroom, flipped off the lights. Hannah snored, John snored, and I listened for a whimper, a whine, until I, too, fell asleep.

Finding a constructive, soulful pathway to tomorrow wasn't easy during the days of missing Sidney, Noah, Lola, and then Orion, but we'd marched on. Probably more accurately, we'd stumbled forward, holding our fears at bay, our hopes close.

If T.S. Eliot (1888–1965) were here, he might have reminded us of this: Though we'd arrived where we started, we knew the place, once more, for the first time.

Twenty-six

MAGIC THINGS

Christmas rolled around with Georgia chewing on John's shoelaces, some washable yard shoes of mine that she faithfully retrieved from my closet every morning, and now and then, puppy Kongs with healthy treats tucked inside. Normally, we had a real tree with all the bright and shiny decorations, but when we received an early holiday gift—a lovely evergreen wreath with battery-operated lights for our front door—we went with that instead.

A puppy and sharp pine needles, after all, weren't the best combination.

Georgia got a new harness for Christmas. At five months, she'd outgrown her first one, and we rarely used traditional collars. When we needed name and vaccination tags, their "official" collars were useful, but otherwise, yanking small necks and heads around never seemed wise. Straining against a leash, which most dogs do sometimes, can cause neck injuries or throat damage. A dog's trachea, or windpipe, when pinched, causes them to choke, cough, or gasp for air. Unpleasant, uncomfortable, at a minimum. Most of us have seen this happen.

What I didn't know, though, before I researched the dangers of collars, was that they can also impact spines, thyroids (located right under many collars), even eyes, to the point of causing glaucoma.

Research points to more physical ailments possibly related to collars: allergies, lung or heart issues, skin or ear conditions, digestive problems, and so on. I also learned that paw licking, often associated with allergies, can, in fact, be linked to leash pulling and/or collar issues that lead to nerve damage and an uncomfortable tingling sensation in the feet. Interesting.

Clearly, a dog's neck is an extremely sensitive area; yet, troubling or dangerous options are out there: choke collars, shock (or vibrating) collars, metal pronged (or pinch) collars. Also available: head collars (Gentle Leader, one brand), martingale collars, show collars, or harnesses (some designed better than others, comfort-wise and safety-wise, and some, for better control, offer a front leash clasp).

Lately "smart collars" (or GPS collars) have arrived on the scene. If they help to find a lost pet, not a bad idea. Anyone tried those yet?

MOST TRAINERS POINT OUT that positive training techniques should always be "first choice." Negative, pain-inducing options that destroy trust quickly make dogs anxious and aggressive, which is plain old common sense. Actual *learning* is something else entirely; learning involves safely, humanely, and patiently teaching new behaviors. Adding pain and stress and fear to an already tense situation is *never* the answer, and merely soothes, temporarily, a distressed, overblown human ego. But patience, a highly desirable trait to cultivate and nurture, facilitates learning. *They help us; we help them.*

Good intentions, consistent follow-through, and a relaxed approach yield caring partnerships, after all. Who knows how many times loyal dogs and cats get us up and moving again—low-energy days, stressful days, or after tragic news hits our ears and hearts. And if it weren't for daily dog walks, would we exercise at all, or might a comfortable couch win out?

I'm afraid many of us know the answer to that one.

Dogs pick *us up* in endless ways: a look, a toy delivered to our hands, dropped by our feet, humorous puppy "zoomies," a rousing game of fetch in the backyard.

Again, I'm struck by these questions. Who is the teacher, the student? Who leans on who? And why is there so much impatience on the human end of things?

Like the speed bumps in Minnesota that frightened Hannah, and our choice to comfort and support her, when we care deeply and pay attention to each moment, each breath, our four-legged family members benefit greatly. *But so do we.* When we give of ourselves in our way, and they give to us in their way, strong and durable bonds develop. Are we worthy of their love and loyalty? Are we truly attentive, or mildly distracted and disinterested?

Sensing and seeing much more than we notice and understand, defenseless animals and pets tolerate quite a bit.

It's my sincere hope that a natural outgrowth of these powerful connections and profound relationships is greater humility. If there is one trait the "human pack" could use more of in nearly any setting, it's the ability to see and empathize with others. Especially, those without a voice.

When it comes to animals, *we are their voice,* but humble and genuine hearts are needed to honor that sacred, and timeless, commitment. Learning, reading, and consulting with wise teachers and mentors, instead of listening exclusively to our old thoughts, tired ideas, and habitual ways of behaving, can also help us become strong and caring advocates for the animals in our care, or otherwise.

For Christmas, Hannah and Georgia also got dog puzzles and fun, "slow feed" dog bowls. Neither of them gulp down their food—Hannah prefers to chew one or two pieces at a time, Georgia takes her time, too—but nonetheless, on days when they seem bored with life or their food, maze bowls are a fun way to offer stimulation.

Hannah's bowl, dishwasher safe, BPA-, PVC- and phthalate-free, resembled a teal maze with ridges; Georgia's bowl, the easiest option, looked like a purple flower. Of course, they were curious, and spent a good ten minutes retrieving their kibble. On a 20-below-zero day with three feet of snow on the ground, the perfect antidote.

The floor puzzles entailed sliding a cover open to find the hidden treat. The super easy version was their favorite, but the most challenging one held their interest the longest. Watching them figure these out was heartwarming. Having "something to do" is important for all of us. A good friend of mine told me they made easy dog jumps for their backyard. Their dogs loved them. (Prebuilt jumps in various sizes are also available from online vendors.) *Another great idea.*

Honoring the energy of other living creatures is not only considerate, it's smart; plus, it's a powerful way to counter our own malcontent natures.

Joan Ranquet, animal communicator and energy healer, teaches nationwide. Her books include: *Energy Healing for Animals: A Hands-On Guide for Enhancing the Health, Longevity & Happiness of Your Pets,* and *Communication with All Life: Revelations of an Animal Communicator.*

Ranquet's website and blog are a goldmine of useful information about her digital courses, workshops, and publications (also on Goodreads).

Learning of her work from my undergraduate alma mater, Stephens College, in Columbia, Missouri, Ranquet graduated from Stephens in 1982, a few years after I did. And in September of 2017, she visited campus to work with equestrian students and interaction techniques with horses.

While at Stephens, Ranquet took time to meet with students fostering pets via a Columbia no-kill shelter. During this session, she talked about how to connect with these animals to "bring out the best in them."

She explained that we do this by getting quiet and tuning in to their energy, and not making negative assumptions. Working with foster dog Coors, a light-colored schnauzer-mix, Ranquet pointed out that it's especially important not to "feel sorry" for them, because they pick up on our feelings and think something is wrong. This, she noted, creates a vicious cycle. Better, Ranquet said, to approach rescues with "fun and confidence."

I'd never thought about this, have you?

"Animals respond to fun faster than anything else," Ranquet added, and when we tap their better qualities, they may get adopted sooner.

That really did make sense.

Cautioning against "projecting the rescue animal mentality on the animal," I liked her suggestion. Plenty of dogs, not even rescues, don't get much fun or play time. Difficult not to feel sorry for them, as well. But when trying to create trust, by giving them safe, varied ways to use plentiful energy reserves—acknowledging innate physical and emotional needs—we promote a respectful and caring relationship. And isn't that really the goal?

CHRISTMAS OF 2018 IS NOW a memory. Time moved on. Georgia, a year old, grew up and into a beautiful gray and white coat with a hint of curl. Bright eyes survey and study everything, including us; she's curious and playful. She doesn't howl at the moon; she howls at sirens. Her bark, if she's especially excited, sounds like a high-pitched squeal, and she loves wool dryer balls, patiently standing by me in the utility room waiting for one to drop. She also likes to catch dragonflies and is especially fond of bookmarks she can pry from our books. Georgia sleeps and plays with sincere abandon, like all the members of our beloved no worries club: *Sidney, Lola, Noah, Orion, and Hannah.*

Tonight, the air is warm and still—an evening with no mosquitoes—so we're in the backyard playing a little fetch with "Chuckit" the "flying squirrel" and Kong "air dogs."

Hannah, already four, and Georgia run and chase, roll and dodge, hop and pounce, like dear old friends, *like sisters*. And I'm reminded of the many changes that have come our way since the dominoes began to fall in 2015 with Noah's June departure: Lola, May of 2017; Orion, late March 2018. Now, with the summer of 2019 upon us, we assume that sweet Georgia is our "last dog."

But is she?

How long will Hannah remain healthy? Or Georgia? What would we do if one or both came down with a serious medical condition tomorrow? I'm not sure.

It's difficult to even consider such a scenario.

Realistically, though, we've learned that the future unfolds in its own way with or without our consent. Things happen. Time runs short. But, for now, watching our "girls" run and play is enough. They have each other; we have them. And as the ever timely Albert Einstein told us: "We are slowed down sound and light waves, a walking bundle of frequencies tuned into the cosmos. We are souls dressed up in sacred biochemical garments and our bodies are the instruments through which our souls play their music."

So here's to the music in all of us. To the art of being and sharing our lives with animals—knowing only brief life spans, and with no choice but to endure whatever life conditions come their way. Their presence, a sparkling gift that often enough we surely don't deserve.

Yet, another day beckons, and many of us hope that the power of our love—time, attention, affection—makes a real difference. That the world our four-legged family members gaze upon from a cozy window seat is safe, welcoming, and trustworthy, because, in all reality, last dogs probably aren't last. And that's a *happy truth*.

Sure, we may *think* they are, but Orion was our first "last dog," Hannah was our second "last dog," and Georgia is our third "last dog." The future is unknowable, and some things in life, like last dogs or last cats, aren't meant to be predicted. It's the fascinating nature of the wheel of time; it has a way of tripping us up, shocking us, and prompting us to grow and learn and continually rethink our "certainties."

As the sun began its daily descent in the western sky, Hannah and Georgia tired and resting on the cool grass, John and I glanced at each other, quietly appreciating the journey that began with our phone-loving white cat, Sidney, and culminated in this very dear moment—and whatever happens next.

Georgia Bliss O'Henri may or may not be the last dog, but four spirited dogs, two clever cats, and fortuitous decisions along the way are *all* valid reasons to celebrate the tremendous intrigue—the deep well of mysteries beyond logic and knowledge, the night sky featuring mesmerizing constellations like Orion—and beauty of life. Even painful losses that show up, unbidden.

As the 1923 winner of the Nobel Prize for Literature, poet and playwright W. B. Yeats, believed, this is a world that's "full of magic things."

Dearest Reader:

Thank you for reading *A Happy Truth*. Would you be so kind as to post a reader comment on Amazon, Goodreads, and other book sites you frequent? **Your opinion, even when brief, is invaluable.** When I consider buying a book, *just like you,* I depend on insightful reader comments to guide my selection. Your help is greatly appreciated. On behalf of myself, and beloved animals the world over that gently remind us all to relax and relinquish our worries, thanks so much!
—*Daisy Hickman*

Orion and the Hibiscus

EPILOGUE

A thing of beauty is a joy for ever:
Its loveliness increases; it will never
Pass into nothingness.
—JOHN KEATS

Signs of Life

The truth is in the red ball,
the way you run and leap,
sniff the air

It's also hiding in your gaze,
your protective bark, your purr,
and most of all, your "tell-all" tail

Ears that perk, droop, flop up
and around when you sail
across a field, but in a flash

A Happy Truth

you pin them back tight to
show us how you feel about
a raging storm, a siren,
a disturbing voice

Monks, wise men, spiritual
gurus, have nothing on you;
women and men of power,
prestige, and royal heritage
pale in your presence

Clouds part, rain dances, trees
bow and sway, flowers open,
in reverence and awe

Such magic in quiet steps
that never stomp or pound
the earth, but gently

you walk the trail of today,
your worries slight, like
dissipating dreams

And when you're gone, harshly silenced,
ears at rest, no longer hearing me,
and honest eyes shuttered

I will miss those signs of life.

—D.A. HICKMAN, *2019*

ZEN OF NOAH RECAP

Many years have flown by since my "Zen of Noah" blog post in *Sunny Room Studio,* so, here, I'd like to step in, once more, as Noah's ghost writer. Like the original post, there's a blend of truth and humor and common sense. To begin, a couple of thought-provoking quotes from Zen Master Dōgen, who lived long ago in Kyoto, Japan (1200–1253).

> Life and death are of supreme importance.
> Time swiftly passes by and opportunity is lost.
> Each of us should strive to awaken. Awaken!
> Take heed, do not squander your life.

> If you are unable to find the truth right where
> you are, where else do you expect to find it?

As I wrote in the "Zen of Noah" chapter, Noah was a relaxed and mellow guy who seemed to *know* things beyond his years and canine heritage. If still with us, here are my thoughts on the tips and ideas—*the humble admissions*—he'd be eager to share with you.

- I wasn't all peaches and cream: One day, I was home alone, got bored and shredded every piece of paper in John's office. *Fun,* but I was young and rowdy then, so please, don't follow in my footsteps.

- Here's a great quote from Abraham Lincoln: "I am in favor of animal rights as well as human rights. That is the way of a whole human being."

- Don't leave animals of any kind—dogs, cats, chickens, horses, cows, birds, and so on—in hot cars or trailers. When you see an animal trapped in a car, window barely cracked (or not at all), report it immediately. Animals can suffer and die this way. It's true. Stay at the scene until the situation is resolved. My friends tell me that even a 78-degree day can, within minutes, turn into 100 degrees in a car; dogs can suffer a heat stroke or brain damage in less than fifteen minutes in such conditions.

- Until we reach our glorious golden years, call us *pet kids;* it has a nice ring to it. Or maybe just kids!

- When things go awry, and most sadly, we must part company, please stay with me at the vet's office until

I'm gone. Not partially gone, as in a deep sleep, but until I'm gone-gone. I need you then more than ever. It's hard, yes, but *you* are my family—in good times and bad, happy and sad. I was lucky; I wasn't alone. It helped so much.

- Speaking of hot cars, what about concrete and asphalt? My bare paws aren't made of trendy silicone; in fact, they are quite sensitive to heat and cold. Did you know, for instance, when it's a pleasant 78 degrees, concrete is 95 and asphalt is 114? Serious burns have happened to some of my friends, because when it's even warmer outside, say 85, sidewalks are 105, streets and parking lots are soaring up to 130. But it gets worse! When it's 91 outside, and we go for a walk down the street, I must brave 125 degrees on my unprotected paws, 140 on asphalt. Grassy pathways are an option. I also love cool evenings and early mornings for strolling together in the summer. As someone super smart once said: *When it's too hot for you, it's too hot for me.*

- Spending time with four-legged family members can become a spiritual practice. After all, we have things to teach our human caretakers and friends. When it looks like we're meditating, maybe we are—that's *our* secret. When we need your patience and kindness and your time (we know you're busy), you might want to see us as "guardians of being," as Eckhart Tolle referred to us in a book about "spiritual teachings from our dogs and cats." Sometimes I think we are the light at the end of the tunnel, don't you? Julie Barton's book,

Dog Medicine: How My Dog Saved Me from Myself, will prove my point. And there are many such stories along those lines.

- Remember, I'm not a stuffed toy and need frequent exercise—it's a dog thing. And just like you, I get bored, so please don't plop me in a crate for endless hours like a prisoner who broke the law. We take it personally, you know! My crate should be a safe, comforting place, where I can go to rest or enjoy some time alone. A good crate pad or bed that's supportive (memory foam helps my joints) is important, especially as I grow old. Large crates are also much better for us. We can stretch, stand, move, roll around! Thanks for your compassion.

- When summer temps soar (or winter roars), and you leave your precious dogs in an outdoor kennel without protection from the elements, my friends are miserable. Plenty of shade and cool water is needed in the summer; a dry, warm bed and an insulated house with access to food and water are a must for winter. But taking your pet kids indoors is really the smartest, kindest option, unless it's a mild, beautiful day.

- Though it's terribly hard to say good-bye to a dog or a cat you've loved, remember, it's hard for us, too. But don't hesitate or wait forever to love again. So many dogs and cats need your love and concern. And because of our unique personalities, each and every pet is "new" and never a replacement for the sweet dog or cat you're missing. Life is short. Don't wait for the perfect moment or the right day of the week. Love while you have the chance. You, only you, can make another dog or cat very happy when you just say ... *yes*.

- Though I'm not a real Zen master, I was a pretty smart dog in my day. So they told me, anyway. I was a good traveler, too. Whenever we went somewhere in the car, I had a good time. But I was a relaxed kind of guy, so I hopped in the front seat, and stretched out for a long nap on John's left leg when he was driving. It was comforting and fun to be with my human family. They loved me, and I had a really good life. For my part, I was patient, loyal, and trustworthy: Definitely what you might call a "good dog." I hope my comforting, joyful presence lives on through other dogs and cats that share their days on Earth with very lucky humans. Take care. —**Love, Noah**

Noah at McCrory Gardens

AUTHOR NOTE

If you're inclined to wonder if *A Happy Truth* only contains dog or cat advice or pet training recommendations of the scientific, medical variety, wonder no more. I wrote this memoir from many years of personal experience, reading and research, and the occasional intuitive nudge. With an academic background in sociology, the life-enhancing and magical role of dogs and cats in a societal and cultural context has been an ongoing interest of mine. Informally, I've studied and observed pets in relation to humans since I was mature enough to grasp relational dynamics.

Integral to the lives of generation upon generation, the immeasurable value of family members with four legs (fewer in some cases, depending on disabilities, accidents, and such) is apparent to many. I'm sure, in fact, you've also noticed how diligently they strive to keep *us* going, comforting and encouraging us through some of our more difficult days. We presume to carry them, but realistically, it's a two-way street.

I see *A Happy Truth* as a timeless celebration of the innumerable animal-friends that not only tolerate us, but, perhaps, even love us—despite inflated egos, accidental or well-meant missteps, and short-sighted ways. Most of us have perceptive, caring hearts, and seeing our lives through "their eyes" is a fascinating endeavor. ALL pets—exotic or mixed-breeds, strays or rescues, cats or dogs—depend on *us* for good homes. Animals, in general, are inevitably at the mercy of the strong, but often mercurial, human heart.

A touch of humility, supported by greater awareness, patience, and genuine concern can enhance their brief lives, and help to rescue innocent animals from a wild and frenzied world that too often forgets, or fails, to care with intention.

Recently, I read a troubling post on Facebook from a canine rescue shelter. Memorial Day weekend had rolled around, and the shelter had been inundated with dogs because of holiday travel. They reported, in fact, that in a single day some 180 dogs were surrendered. Their owners were leaving town, didn't want to pay boarding, and said they would just get a "new dog" when they returned. The post implored readers to help because they were full and couldn't keep all of the surrendered pets. Mentioning the need for new homes where the dogs would be "family" and not something "disposable," the picture I caught was of a scared-looking puppy: a schnauzer of only thirteen weeks. We can do better; we must do better.

WARM THANKS

First of all, a special mention to the tireless, caring, and knowledgeable veterinarians we've had the privilege to know because of our cats and dogs. Whether keeping our "friends and family" healthy and safe, offering advice and support whenever needed, or just listening to our concerns, these opportunities for connection have been a deeply appreciated aspect of the journey. Coping with emergency challenges, thankless hours, and difficult situations are inherent to this profession; yet, it can't be easy, so *thank you* for all you do. Because of your dedication to the animals and pets we, and many others, have come to love, you make the world a far better place. *Special thanks* to gifted veterinarians who have touched our lives: Dr. Frank Quattrocchi, Dr. Betty Kramek, Dr. Adam Benson, Dr. Jill Hyland Ayres.

Along these lines, I'd like to acknowledge Steph, our dedicated pet groomer. Because she was sensitive to their fears, personalities, and quirks, all four of our dogs have benefited from her generous affection, knowledge, and skills. Grateful for her strong commitment to dogs, we love her warm personality and appreciate her friendship. In the end, you can't ever fool a dog. Keen judges of both character and genuine kindness, Steph always wins them over.

Also, my heartfelt appreciation to patient and perceptive early readers, the staff at 1106 Design—*thank you, Michele and Ronda*—and everyone else offering ideas or feedback along the way. Special thanks to Susan Pohlman for her thoughtful and generous foreword. I've had the pleasure of following her work since I discovered her wonderful memoir, *Halfway to Each Other: How a Year in Italy Brought Our Family Home*. Also an editor and writing coach, for more information, here's Susan's website: https://www.susanpohlman.com.

And to sweet Hannah, thank you for gracing the cover of this book—you and your spinach—and for the countless times you make us smile each day. You're the dog that almost wasn't; yet, the same dog that inspired this book and led us to a happy truth: Last dogs aren't always last. A pure joy, a family member with the most beautiful eyes and spirit, Hannah Rose Leia was the perfect name for you.

Finally, a word of gratitude to tolerant companions of the four-legged variety the world over. Perhaps, *you* hold the key to unlocking the human spirit. Something tells me you do.

If we can't learn to treat those without a real voice as "kindred spirits," perhaps, we won't ever be able to see the way forward: an inspired path that acknowledges and understands the deep connection uniting all life forms. Learning to care proactively for defenseless animals, those invited into our homes, those forced to endure hot or frigid temperatures in crowded, grassless feedlots, small pens or cages, in consistently humane and sensitive ways may be the *real* classroom on our fragile planet. So it seems.

ABOUT THE AUTHOR

D. A. (Daisy) Hickman, an avid and engaged observer of culture and society, writes to connect more deeply to the complexities of the human condition. Her work is inspired by the natural world, spirituality, and an ongoing search for a deeper perspective. With an academic background in sociology, Hickman believes that the collective story is as profound and fascinating as the individual story.

Her memoir, *The Silence of Morning: A Memoir of Time Undone,* followed a first book from William Morrow about growing up "prairie-wise" (*Always Returning: The Wisdom of Place,* second edition).

Also a poet, in 2017, Hickman published *Ancients of the Earth: Poems of Time.* "All too often," she notes, "we manage to give our lives to *time,* but most would agree, it's the wrong emphasis." One of her favorite poems from *Ancients* is "The Art of Remembering."

Hickman studied sociology (M.S.) at Iowa State University and legal studies (B.A.) at Stephens College. A longtime member of the Academy of American Poets and the South Dakota State Poetry Society, Hickman's blog and website, SunnyRoomStudio.com, is a welcoming and inspiring space for kindred spirits.

Additionally, the author has worked extensively with nonprofit organizations. Hickman's expertise is in complex organization, i.e., fund development, leadership and management transitions, organizational planning, evolution, and development.

Follow the author on her SunnyRoomStudio Facebook page, on Twitter @dhsunwriter, on Goodreads, or contact her via email: wisdom@sunnyroomstudio.com.

At work on a new poetry collection, *Sometimes We Fly*, the author lives with her husband, John, and their sweet, spirited schnauzers, Hannah and Georgia.

Ancients of the Earth: Poems of Time (2017)

The Silence of Morning: A Memoir of Time Undone (2015)

Always Returning: The Wisdom of Place (2014)

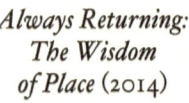

For more about Hickman's books, content descriptions and reviews are available on Amazon and Goodreads. Also, please visit SunnyRoomStudio.com for additional information.

www.ingramcontent.com/pod-product-compliance
Lightning Source LLC
Chambersburg PA
CBHW020417010526
44118CB00010B/300